ENEMY
OF THE PEOPLE

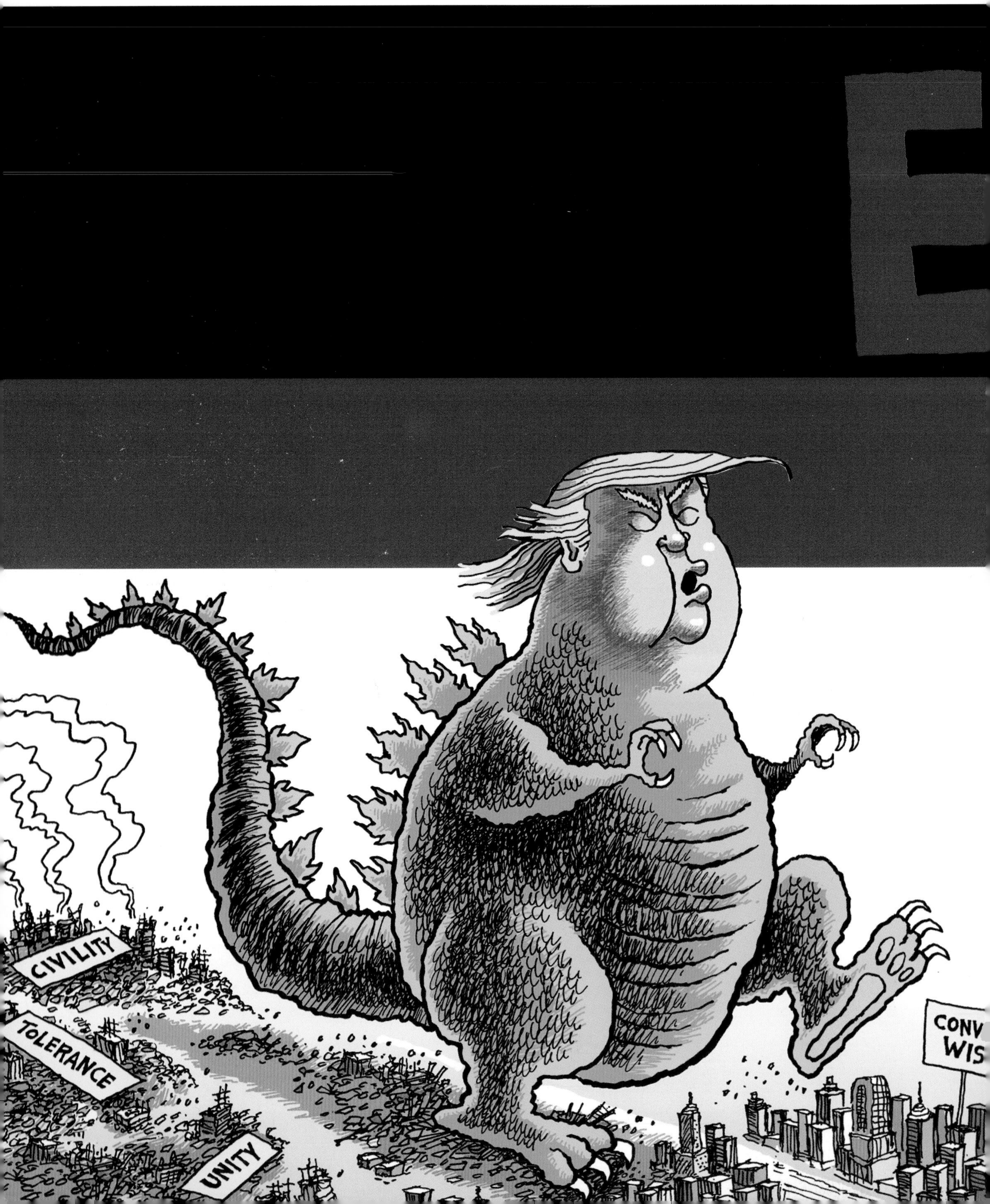
E
CIVILITY
TOLERANCE
UNITY
CONV
WIS

NEMY
OF THE PEOPLE

A CARTOONIST'S JOURNEY
BY ROB ROGERS

IDW

Facebook: **facebook.com/idwpublishing**
Twitter: **@idwpublishing**
YouTube: **youtube.com/idwpublishing**
Tumblr: **tumblr.idwpublishing.com**
Instagram: **instagram.com/idwpublishing**

ISBN : 978-1-68405-594-4   22 21 20 19

WRITTEN AND ILLUSTRATED BY
ROB ROGERS

EDITED BY
TOM WASELESKI

COLLECTION EDITED BY
JUSTIN EISINGER

DESIGNED BY
RICHARD SHEINAUS
FOR **GOTHAM DESIGN**

Special Thanks to: Tom Waseleski, David Fitzsimmons, Dennis Roddy, Steve Brodner, Ann Telnaes, Joel Pett, Pat Bagley, Andy Marlette, Sanjit Sethi and the Association of American Editorial Cartoonists.

Chris Ryall, *President & Publisher/CCO*
John Barber, *Editor-in-Chief*
Robbie Robbins, *EVP/Sr. Art Director*
Cara Morrison, *Chief Financial Officer*
Matt Ruzicka, *Chief Accounting Officer*
Anita Frazier, *SVP of Sales and Marketing*
David Hedgecock, *Associate Publisher*
Jerry Bennington, *VP of New Product Development*
Lorelei Bunjes, *VP of Digital Services*
Justin Eisinger, *Editorial Director, Graphic Novels & Collections*
Eric Moss, *Senior Director, Licensing and Business Development*

Ted Adams, *Founder*

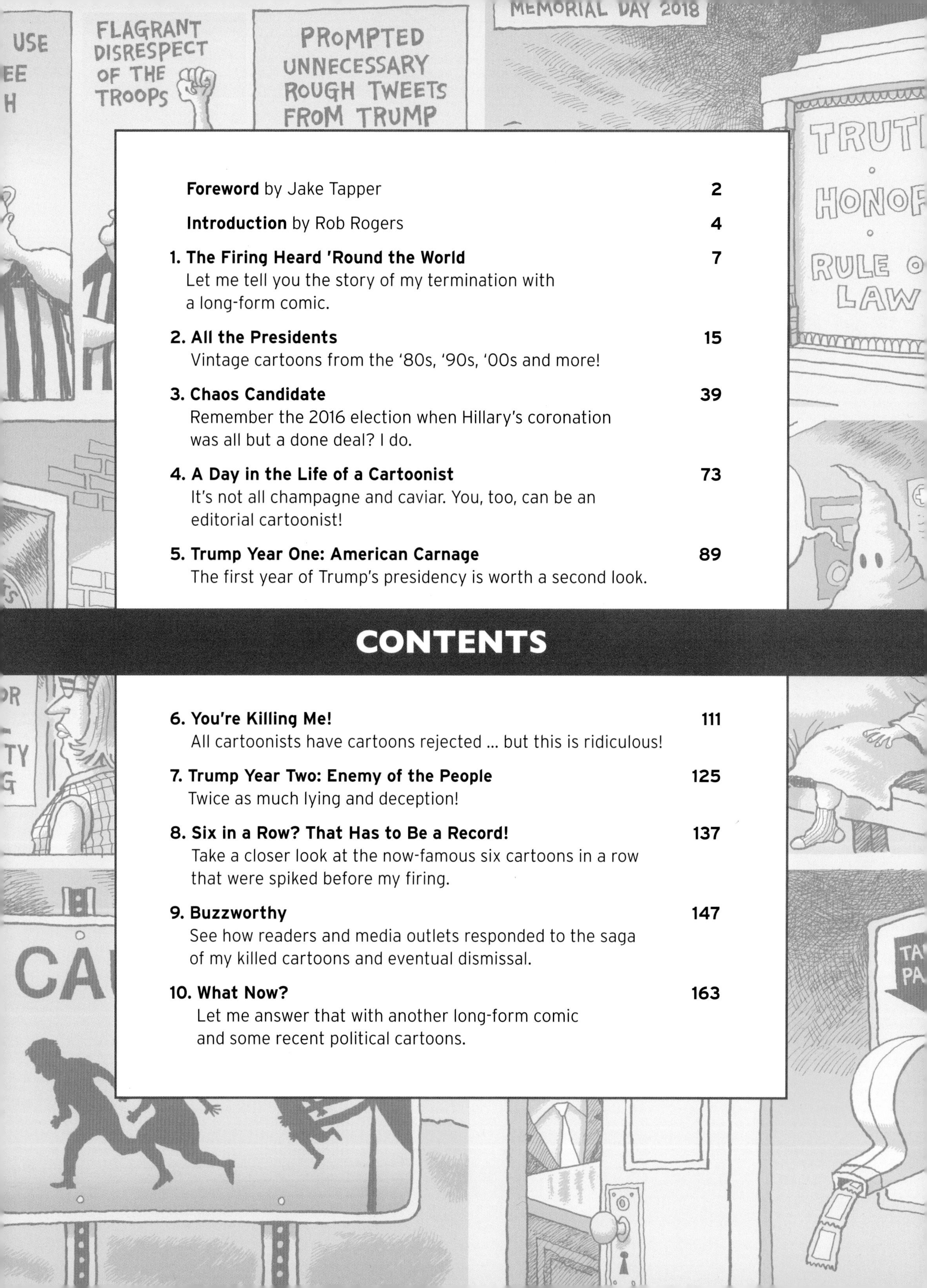
FLAGRANT DISRESPECT OF THE TROOPS
PROMPTED UNNECESSARY ROUGH TWEETS FROM TRUMP
MEMORIAL DAY 2018

CONTENTS

Foreword

Humans have been caricaturing and mocking our leaders almost certainly since art began, though scholars trace the history of political cartoons back to James Gillray, who skewered King George III in the 1700s. A century later, Thomas Nast became the founding father of the form in the United States, with his devastating portraits of Boss Tweed and the corrupt Tammany Hall machine.

All of which is a fancy way of saying that editorial cartoons have been an indispensable part of how the West has emerged as a beacon of liberty and freedom: Political cartoonists have been there speaking truth to power all the way. It's difficult to think of Richard Nixon without regarding the cartoons of Paul Conrad and Herblock; Jimmy Carter and Ronald Reagan also need to be seen in the work of Pat Oliphant and Jeff MacNelly. And so on.

The terrain today for political cartoonists has sadly become a difficult one, what with the struggles of newspapers in an increasingly digital age, but these important satirists continue to ink up a storm, amuse us and outrage us, highlighting the foibles and hypocrisies of the mess of democracy.

Rob Rogers has stood for more than a quarter-century as one of the more gifted political cartoonists – with awards to spare, loyal local and national followings, a taste for the jugular and a quill aimed at the powerful.

Unfortunately for readers of the *Pittsburgh Post-Gazette*, the publisher and editor-in-chief, John Robinson Block, does not seem to appreciate the role of political cartoonists in our society, particularly the need for them to be independent voices.

Block proudly wears his support for the most powerful person in the world. After a Trump rally in 2016, Block met with candidate Trump on his campaign plane where he took a chummy photograph with him, one he posted on Facebook with the caption: "In 39 years of full-time journalism I've met many interesting people. This one was more than memorable."

Publishers and editors have opinions, of course, and no one should begrudge Block exercising his right as an American to express his, on Facebook or on the pages of his newspaper.

What is regrettable is that the aptly-named Block soon enough prevented Rogers from expressing *his* views where he had done so for a quarter-century. After a period where the paper's new editorial director, Keith Burris, censored Rogers' cartoons from the newspaper and urged him to be less pointed and focus on other

targets instead of Trump, Rogers was shown the door.

Block later told *Politico* he thought Rogers had "become too angry for his health or for his own good. He's obsessed with Trump."

To be fair to Block and Burris, they run a newspaper in a world where newspaper readership is dwindling and, while Pittsburgh is not exactly a Trump stronghold, Trump won all of the surrounding counties and the commonwealth of Pennsylvania as a whole.

That said, Block's criticism is confounding.

Political cartoonists are *supposed* to be angry. Political cartoonists are *supposed* to obsess about people in power.

Whether conservative cartoonists angry with Barack Obama and obsessing over Hillary Clinton, or progressive ones angry with Trump and obsessing over him, this is what they are supposed to do.

In a world where corporate chefs tend to take anything with flavor and water it down into bland gruel, it is disappointing that Burris and Block would not cherish and protect this outspoken and celebrated independent editorial voice.

It is sadly not news that people who run corporations are often more comfortable with fealty to power than righteous indignation against it. Yet that is precisely the opposite of what journalism is supposed to be. As Thomas Jefferson once wrote, "were it left to me to decide whether we should have a government without newspapers, or newspapers without a government, I should not hesitate a moment to prefer the latter."

With power comes accountability and mockery, however much the president's Praetorian Guard would have it otherwise.

Kindly enjoy this book of cartoons celebrating the fact that our Founding Fathers understood this, even if others sadly do not.

– **Jake Tapper**
Anchor of "The Lead" and "State of the Union" on CNN

Introduction

In case you haven't heard, I'm the guy who got fired. More specifically, I'm the political cartoonist who, after a 25-year career at the *Pittsburgh Post-Gazette*, was fired for drawing unflattering cartoons about President Trump. In other words, I was fired for doing my job.

I am not the first cartoonist to be fired and I won't be the last. Editorial cartoonists have experienced downsizing since the 1990s. Newspapers have struggled for decades to survive in an ever-changing news delivery landscape. Declining readership and ad revenue have led to the decimation of newsrooms across the country, often resulting in the elimination of the editorial cartoonist position. Strictly from an economic standpoint, I am surprised I lasted as long as I did. My firing was not the result of a penny-pinching move.

I'm also not the first Pennsylvania cartoonist to face serious opposition.

When Republican Samuel W. Pennypacker ran for governor in 1902, he became highly annoyed by a series of political cartoons printed in the *North American* out of Philadelphia. According to historian Steven L. Piott of Clarion University of Pennsylvania, cartoonist Charles Nelan repeatedly drew Pennypacker as a preening parrot. Pennypacker won the election but the cartoons continued. On January 28, 1903, Republican Representative Frederick Taylor Pusey introduced an "anti-cartoon" bill in the state legislature that made it illegal to draw a cartoon depicting a person as a bird, fish, insect or other animal. But the cartoonists were too smart for the lawmakers. They began drawing politicians, especially Pennypacker, as inanimate objects—trees, beer steins and turnips. That's right, turnips. The bill was ridiculed and never passed.

But that didn't stop Pennypacker. A few weeks later, the legislature passed a broader bill, the Salus-Grady libel law, better known as the Pennsylvania anti-cartoon law. Pennypacker signed the bill into law on May 12, 1903. The law expanded the terms under which a newspaper could be sued for libel and made editors themselves the targets for lawsuits. Rather than discourage the production of cartoons, the law only encouraged newspapers to push back harder and caused cartoonists to create even more scathing caricatures. The anti-cartoon law went mostly unenforced until it was abolished in 1907.

This is not 1903 and my "Pennypacker" is not a governor. He's a publisher. My former publisher, that is. A publisher more than happy to carry out the unspoken wishes of our press-hating president. This should be extremely alarming to citizens everywhere. It is bad enough that news organizations such as Sinclair Media and Fox News act like shills for the president and give credence to his conspiracy theories and lies. It is even more disturbing when a previously respected left-leaning newspaper, which just celebrated its 232nd birthday, tosses tradition, precedent, truth and quality journalism in the dumpster and reimagines itself as an arm of the Trump White House.

It wasn't always this way. As I look back on my career I am more awed by the cartoons my newspaper allowed me to draw than by the ones they rejected. For decades the *Post-Gazette* had the courage to print edgy, controversial cartoons that pushed the boundaries and really made readers think. They defended my work and stood behind me. I will always be grateful and humbled by that.

Let's consider the bigger picture: This is not about me losing my job. The important take-away here is that Trump's open embrace of the darkest, ugliest corners of human nature has emboldened racists, neo-Nazis, criminals, thugs, despots, misogynists and liars to come out from under their rocks and display their shameful behavior publicly. That includes publishers and editors who years ago may have been too ashamed to express their hateful views on the editorial page. We are living

in a cockeyed world where someone who tells the truth is seen as part of the resistance, where a reporter from *The New York Times* is suddenly a freedom fighter.

I am proud of the work I have done. I wake up every morning excited to fight the good fight, to afflict the comfortable, to speak truth to power and, yes, to make people laugh. I love what I do and I have no plans to stop now.

I will begin by drawing Trump as a turnip!

– Rob Rogers

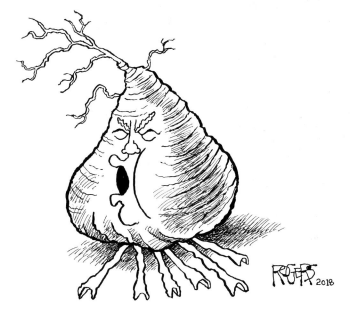

Tom Waseleski, June 15, 2018

Rob Rogers is one of the finest editorial cartoonists working in the country today. I should know — I was his boss for 12 years. Don't believe the claims about why Rob was fired — the claims by the *Post-Gazette* that he was unwilling to "collaborate" on his work and ideas. The firing always was and still is about Donald Trump and the publisher's fealty to him.

It has nothing to do with collaboration, unless you count the publisher's desire for Rob to collaborate on muting his criticism of Trump and altering his long-held political views. But think about it. No one asks George Will to collaborate and turn his views liberal or E.J. Dionne to collaborate and turn conservative - not for any editor, not for any publisher. It's a matter of journalistic integrity.

That's why in January 2016, when the publisher demanded that I, as editorial page editor, begin to shift the *Post-Gazette* editorial board and its opinions toward the positions of candidate Trump, I refused. Two months later the deputy editorial page editor and I left the newspaper by choice. Now the body count has risen with the loss of Rob Rogers.

More than political stance, more than opinion section "collaboration," what the owners of the *Post-Gazette* should focus on is whether these departures, because of their personal fascination with Donald Trump, have tarnished the credibility and trustworthiness of the paper's very soul, the editorial page.

Rob stood up for what he believed in and was willing to risk his job to maintain his integrity and the integrity of his profession. In a world where too many news organizations seek to become mouthpieces for specific political ideologies or specific politicians, such as the current president, we need more editorial cartoonists like Rob — cartoonists unafraid to pay a high price for the freedom to express themselves.

Tom Waseleski was an award-winning member of the *Pittsburgh Post-Gazette* Editorial Board from 1990 until 2016 and president of the National Conference of Editorial Writers. The original version of this appeared on Facebook. Minor additions were made for this publication.

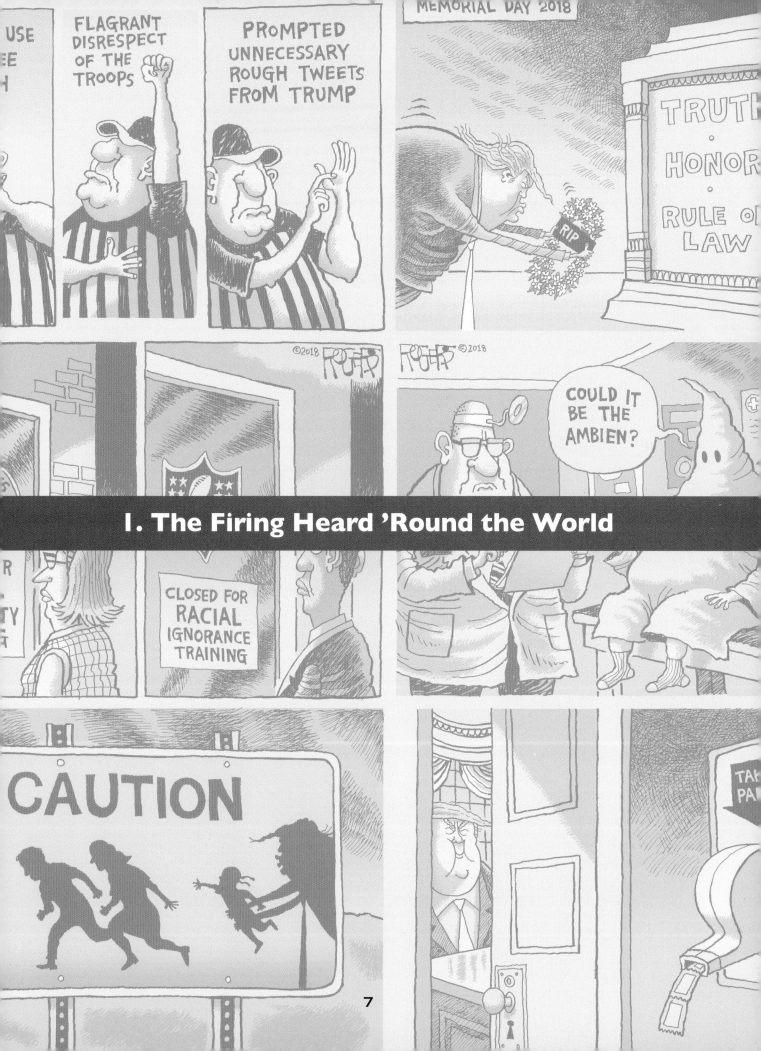

I. The Firing Heard 'Round the World

"**D**o I need to draw you a picture?" is usually not a kind response. It usually means you think someone is too dense to understand your words as spoken. For someone like me, who likes to draw, it may also be a preferred form of communication.

I often found myself thinking those very words when I was describing my firing to people. I could see the puzzled look on their faces as I explained how my publisher was upset with me because I was drawing political cartoons critical of the president. They couldn't comprehend how this could happen.

Maybe you're having trouble understanding it, too. Let me draw you a picture!

DONALD TRUMP COST ME MY JOB...

YOU'RE FIRED!

©2018 ROGERS

OK... HE DIDN'T ACTUALLY SAY THAT TO ME... BUT HE MIGHT AS WELL HAVE...

YOU'RE FIRED!

AFTER **25** YEARS AS THE POLITICAL CARTOONIST FOR THE **PITTSBURGH POST-GAZETTE**, I WAS FIRED IN JUNE FOR BEING TOO CRITICAL OF THE **PRESIDENT.**

WE'RE GONNA NEED YOUR BADGE AND YOUR PEN!

PG

I STARTED MY CAREER AT THE **PITTSBURGH PRESS** IN **1984** WHEN **REAGAN** WAS RUNNING FOR HIS SECOND TERM.

GRECIAN FORMULA

EARLY ON, I WAS STILL LEARNING HOW TO BE A DAILY CARTOONIST. I SHOWED MY EDITOR SEVERAL SKETCHES A DAY.

THESE SUCK! A SIX-YEAR-OLD COULD DO BETTER!

AFTER MY SECOND YEAR, WHEN IT WAS CLEAR THAT I HAD LEARNED TO BE MY OWN BEST **EDITOR,** I WAS GIVEN TOTAL **FREEDOM.**

THESE SUCK! A SIX-YEAR-OLD COULD DO BETTER!

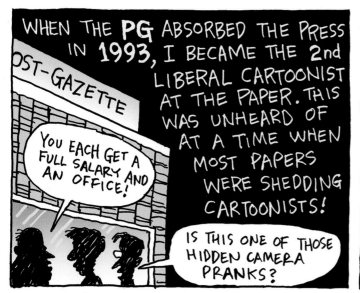

WHEN THE **PG** ABSORBED THE PRESS IN **1993**, I BECAME THE **2nd** LIBERAL CARTOONIST AT THE PAPER. THIS WAS UNHEARD OF AT A TIME WHEN MOST PAPERS WERE SHEDDING CARTOONISTS!

YOU EACH GET A FULL SALARY AND AN OFFICE!

IS THIS ONE OF THOSE HIDDEN CAMERA PRANKS?

I WORKED WELL WITH MY EDITORS, ALWAYS ENGAGING IN A HEALTHY GIVE AND TAKE. LIKE MOST CARTOONISTS, I HAD **2** OR **3** CARTOONS KILLED A YEAR.

SORRY... YOU CAN'T DRAW THE POPE SHITTING IN THE WOODS FOR A FAMILY NEWSPAPER!

THE **PG** HAS ALWAYS BEEN A LEFT-LEANING PAPER. THE PUBLISHER, **JOHN ROBINSON BLOCK** (OR J.R.), MOSTLY KEPT HIS POLITICS TO HIMSELF.

LIBERAL RAG!

POST-GAZETTE

IN 2015, THAT BEGAN TO CHANGE. SUDDENLY, **J.R.** WAS ENAMORED WITH CANDIDATE **TRUMP** AND STARTED HINTING ABOUT A POSSIBLE ENDORSEMENT.

WHAT ABOUT THE MORAL STANDS WE'VE TAKEN FOR DECADES?

WHADDA **WE** KNOW?

PITTSBURGH POST-GAZ

J.R. BEGAN TO PUSH BACK ON MY CARTOONS ABOUT **THE DONALD**.

TELL ROGERS HIS CARTOONS DON'T CAPTURE TRUMP'S INTOXICATING MASCULINITY!

MY EDITORIAL PAGE EDITOR, WHO CHAMPIONED AND DEFENDED ME TO **MANAGEMENT**, TOOK A BUYOUT IN **2016** RATHER THAN ENDORSE DONALD TRUMP.

I'M SO ALONE.

THEN, IN JANUARY 2018, KEITH BURRIS, FROM OUR SISTER PAPER IN TOLEDO, PENNED WHAT MANY CALLED A RACIST DEFENSE OF **TRUMP'S** "SHITHOLE" COMMENTS.

AND HERE I WAS JUST READING FOR THE STEELERS COVERAGE!

POST-GAZETTE
HAPPY MLK DAY!
INSIDE: RACISM

RATHER THAN RETREAT IN SHAME, **J.R.** DOUBLED DOWN BY PROMOTING **BURRIS** TO EDITORIAL DIRECTOR OVER BOTH PAPERS. THE AUTHOR OF "REASON AS RACISM" WAS NOW MY BOSS!

DEAD CARTOONIST DRAWING...

I BEGAN TO ENVISION THE TWO OF THEM AS **MASTER BLASTER** FROM **MAD MAX:** BEYOND THUNDERDOME.

SEVERAL CARTOON IDEAS ENTER, _NO_ CARTOON IDEAS LEAVE!

MASTER BLOCK

BLASTER BURRIS

I WOULD EMAIL MY IDEA TO **J.R.** AND **KEITH** IN THE MORNING... OFTEN BEING FORCED TO REWORK IDEAS ON DEADLINE.

NO!
NO!
GOD, NO!

WITH **BURRIS** I FELT MORE BULLIED THAN MANAGED. HE CALLED MY IDEAS TOO MALICIOUS AND WOULD LECTURE ME ON WHAT MADE GOOD SATIRE.

CONSIDER THE BRILLIANT PRO-SLAVERY CARTOONS OF THE 1850s ... NOW THAT'S SOME SATIRE!

MY BOSSES SAID MY CARTOONS WERE **"NOT FUNNY."** MAYBE THEY WEREN'T LAUGHING BECAUSE THEY WERE SEEING THEIR OWN BELIEFS LAID BARE ON THE EDITORIAL PAGE.

AMBIEN IS FUNNY... BUT WHY TRASH THE KKK?

IN THE THREE MONTHS **BURRIS** WAS MY EDITOR, **19** OF MY CARTOONS OR IDEAS WERE **KILLED.** THE LAST **SIX** WERE IN A ROW. A SOCIAL MEDIA PROTEST BEGAN TO BUILD...

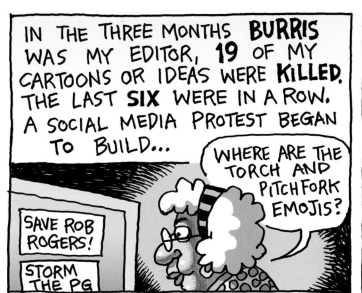

WHERE ARE THE TORCH AND PITCHFORK EMOJIS?

SAVE ROB ROGERS!

STORM THE PG

IT WAS CLEAR FROM THE "WORKING GUIDELINES" CONTRACT THEY ASKED ME TO SIGN THAT THEY WEREN'T INTERESTED IN **WORKING IT OUT.**

I CAN'T WORK THIS WAY!

10 DAYS LATER THEY OFFERED ME AN EQUALLY INSULTING SEVERANCE AGREEMENT THAT DEMANDED THE RIGHTS TO ALL OF MY **CARTOONS.** MY LABOR LAWYER WAS STUNNED.

I'VE FOUGHT MINING COMPANIES THAT KILL PEOPLE... AND THESE ARE THE WORST LABOR DOCUMENTS I'VE EVER SEEN!

SO... YOU PROBABLY FIGURED OUT FROM READING THIS THAT I **DIDN'T** SIGN THE ONEROUS **NON-DISPARAGEMENT AGREEMENT.***

THE NIB

☆@#% ... I GUESS HE DIDN'T SIGN.

THAT'S WHAT **POLITICAL CARTOONISTS** DO... WE DISPARAGE THOSE IN POWER! ESPECIALLY THOSE WHO **ABUSE** THAT POWER!

FORGET BABY PRISONS... WE NEED THOSE CAGES FOR CARTOONISTS!

NOW I'M UNEMPLOYED, BUT ON THE BRIGHT SIDE... THERE'S NO ONE LEFT TO **REJECT** MY CARTOONS!

YOU SUCK!

☆@#% YOU, SNOWFLAKE!

BURN IN **HELL!**

TERRIBLE CARTOONS!

WHERE'D YOU LEARN TO DRAW?

✱ HEY, LAWYERS... ALL DIALOGUE IS SATIRE!

This comic first appeared on The Nib.
www.thenib.com

David Fitzsimmons, June 16, 2018

On Thursday morning my friend, the internationally syndicated cartoonist Rob Rogers, sent out this tweet: "Sad to report this update: Today, after 25 years as the editorial cartoonist for the *Pittsburgh Post-Gazette*, I was fired."

By the time I bounced to Rob's Facebook page to offer condolences, his post already had a gazillion shares and hundreds of comments. Many were from fans who had canceled their subscriptions to the *Post-Gazette* in response to the firing of their favorite editorial cartoonist: "Last *Post Gazette* for me. So long *PG*. Hello *New York Times*," said one.

At the turn of the last century, America's press employed thousands of political cartoonists. Today, as our nation slides into the grip of an authoritarian nationalist who despises the press, there are fewer than 40 of us inking truth to power. And as newspapers perish, and news deserts form and well-funded partisan propagandists fill the void, the old school ink slingers, muckrakers and watchdogs continue to shrink in number.

These are perilous times for voices like Rob Rogers. As the president's ratings creep up, the lickspittles in Congress line up to kiss Trump's ring, the right-wing media machine beats its mighty chest and the president's satirical critics are hammered, I wish the talented Mr. Rogers continued success in spite of the terrible challenges ahead. The same goes for our democratic republic.

David Fitzsimmons is *The Arizona Daily Star*'s editorial cartoonist and weekly humor columnist. His cartoons are globally syndicated through **cagletoons.com.**

2. All The Presidents

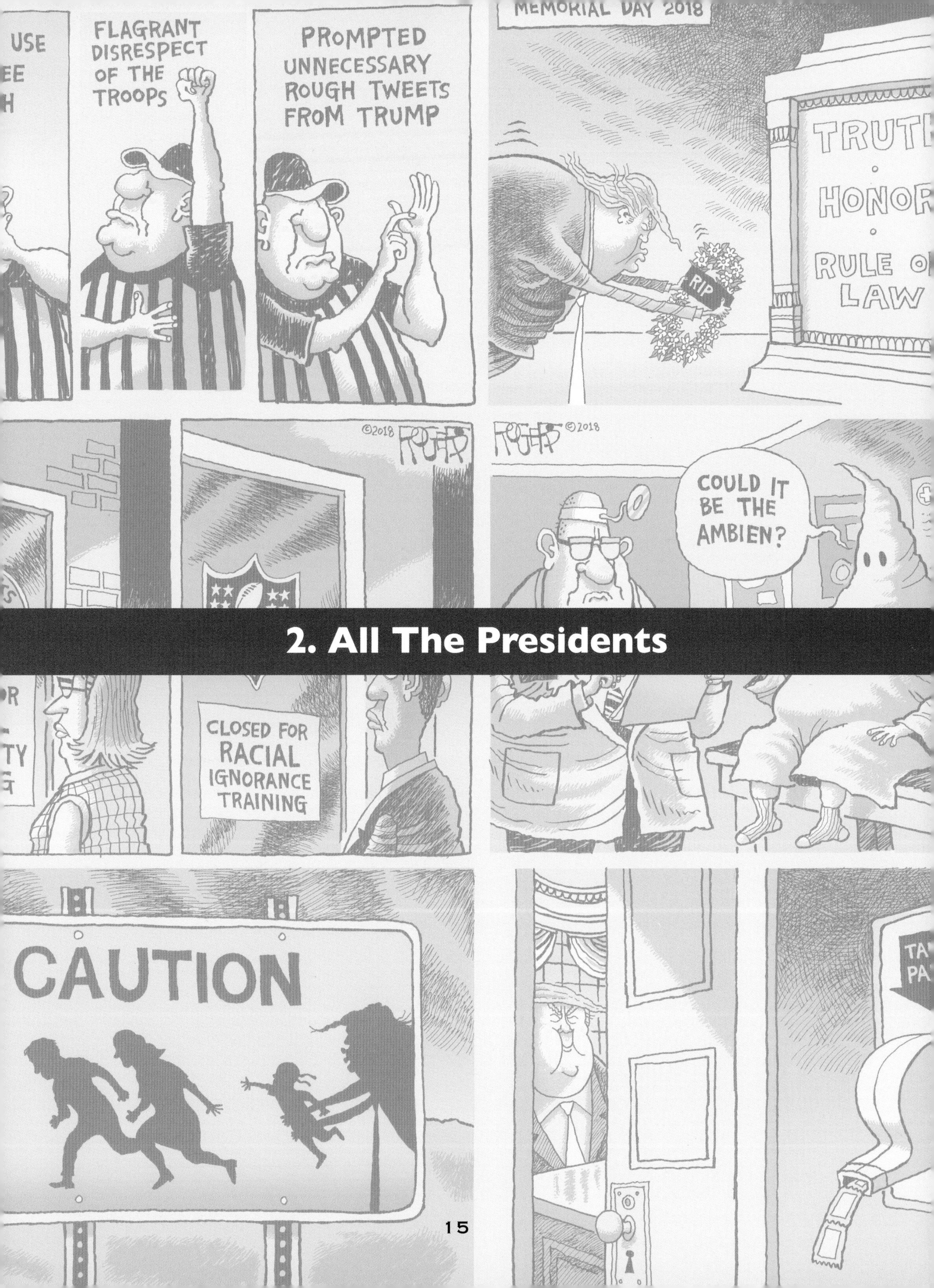
FLAGRANT DISRESPECT OF THE TROOPS
PROMPTED UNNECESSARY ROUGH TWEETS FROM TRUMP
MEMORIAL DAY 2018
RIP
TRUTH
HONOR
RULE OF LAW
©2018 ROGERS
ROGERS ©2018
COULD IT BE THE AMBIEN?
CLOSED FOR RACIAL IGNORANCE TRAINING
CAUTION

Since I was fired for drawing cartoons about the president, I thought it might be apropos to point out that before Donald Trump was elected I had already covered five presidents in my career.

Five. Over three decades.

I started in 1984 at *The Pittsburgh Press* drawing cartoons about Ronald Reagan's re-election campaign. Then I drew cartoons about George H.W. Bush, Bill Clinton, George W. Bush and Barack Obama.

Not once during those 32 years was I ever fired for drawing cartoons about the president. Why? Because it was my job!

Here are some of those other presidents.

During a sound check before taping one of his Saturday radio addresses, President Reagan joked that the U.S. would begin bombing Russia in five minutes. – *August 15, 1984*

Reagan's Cold War rhetoric was infused with the movie jargon of the day: "Star Wars" was his nickname for a missile defense system and "Evil Empire" was his tag for the Soviet Union. – *December 26, 1984*

Reagan declared that since the SALT II Treaty's missile limits were being ignored by the Soviets, the U.S. would do the same. – *January 1, 1986*

Although Reagan faced repeated thorny questions about the Iran-Contra scandal, nothing seemed to stick to the Teflon president. – *January 3, 1986*

Like many conservatives, Reagan believed in deep cuts to domestic programs but lavish
spending on the military. - *February 4, 1986*

Democrats were furious that money from U.S. arms sales to Iran was being secretly funneled
to the right-wing Contra rebels in Nicaragua. - *March 21, 1986*

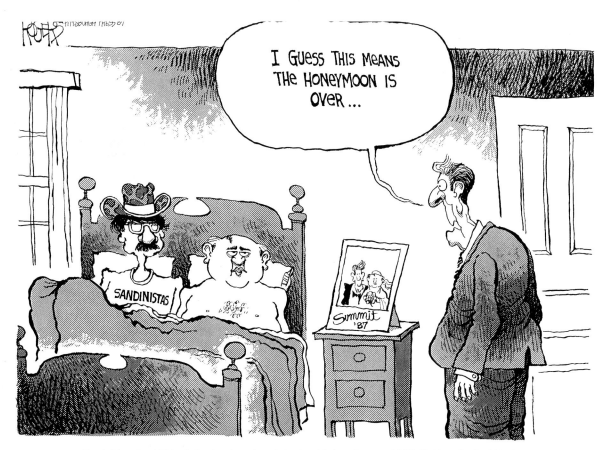

Soviet leader Mikhail Gorbachev, in a televised interview on NBC, flatly rejected that the U.S. could be threatened by Nicaragua's Marxist Sandinista regime. - *January 6, 1987*

President Reagan was given to memory lapses when faced with questions about approving the sale of arms to Iran. - *January 8, 1987*

Weeks after Michael Jackson released his mega-selling album *Bad*, Vice President George H.W. Bush tried to toughen his image for a 1988 run for president. – *October 14, 1987*

Republicans were more concerned about flag burnings than cross burnings.
– *June 29, 1989*

Vice President Dan Quayle became a regular source of embarrassment for President Bush.
- *July 23, 1989*

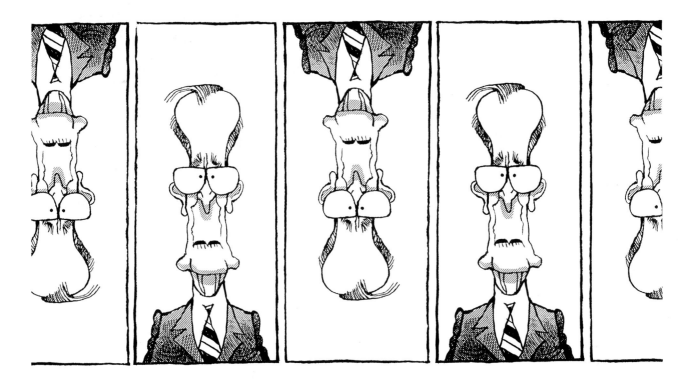

GEORGE BUSH ON TAXES

So much for Bush's "Read my lips" anti-tax promise from the campaign.
- *October 11, 1990*

By attacking Iraq after it invaded Kuwait, the president went back on a warning he had given aggressive nations. - *January 20, 1991*

As the bombs burst overhead during the U.S.-led coalition's liberation of Kuwait from Iraq, troops had a new understanding of the Bush slogan about community volunteers. - *January 22, 1991*

President Bush got plenty of mileage from the brief war with Iraq.
- *January 31, 1991*

Unfortunately for Bush, Iraqi President Saddam Hussein stuck around, just like the U.S. recession.
- *January 29, 1992*

Pressure mounted for a special prosecutor to be appointed by the Justice Department to investigate Bill and Hillary Clinton's Whitewater investments in Arkansas. - *January 11, 1994*

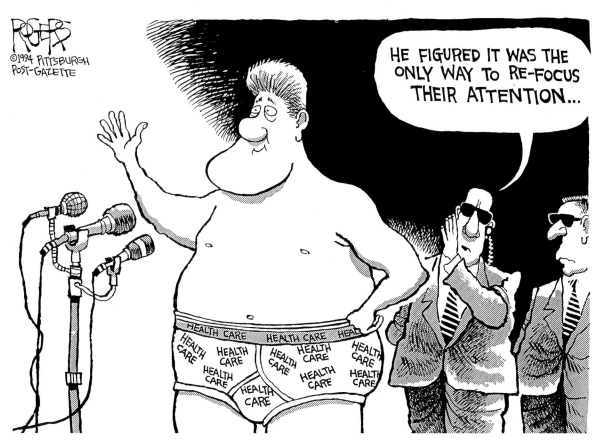

The Paula Jones sexual harassment lawsuit, the Whitewater probe and other issues became stumbling blocks for Clinton on passing a health care plan. - *May 24, 1994*

Bill Clinton couldn't seem to shake the scandal cloud that followed him.
- *July 16, 1994*

Adding to Clinton's headaches was the story that overnight stays in the Lincoln Bedroom
were offered to political donors. - *January 30, 1997*

While news of Clinton's affair with Monica Lewinsky threatened to destroy his presidency, Americans were pleased on other fronts. - *January 25, 1998*

In the face of multiple scandals, Clinton tried to look presidential.
- *January 27, 1998*

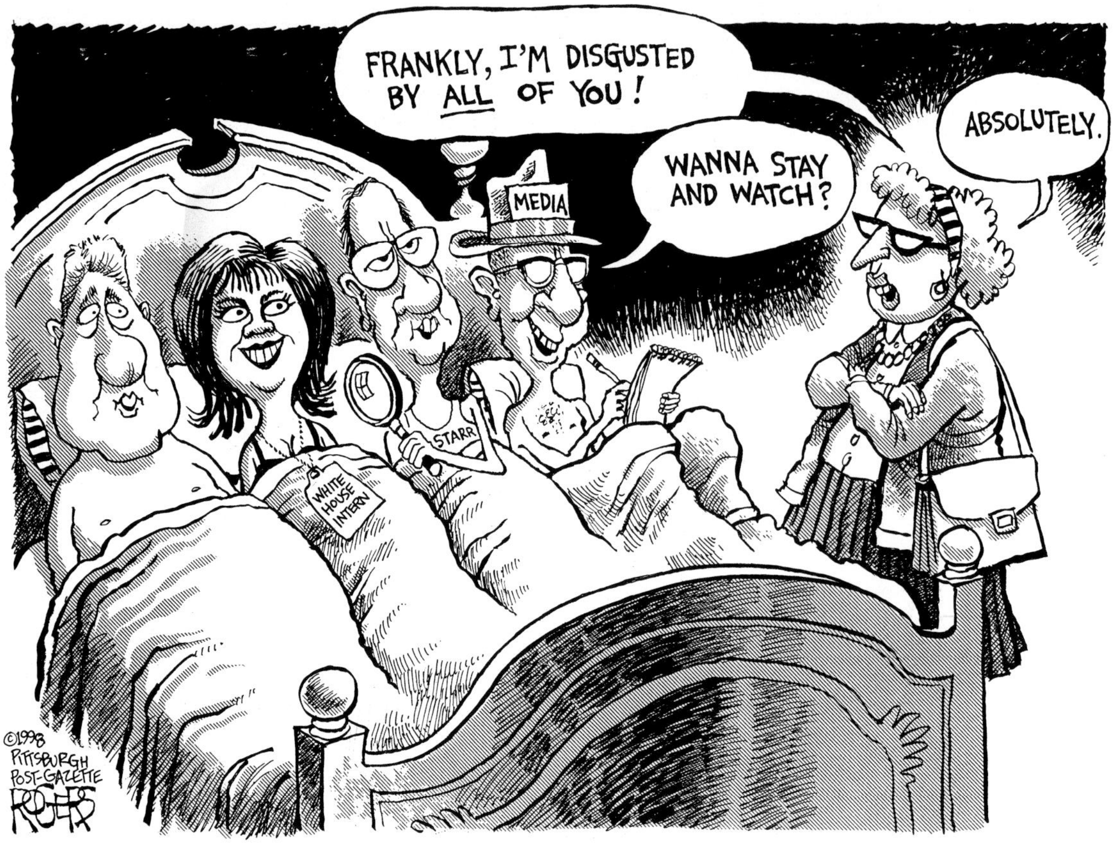
FRANKLY, I'M DISGUSTED BY ALL OF YOU!
WANNA STAY AND WATCH?
ABSOLUTELY.
MEDIA
WHITE HOUSE INTERN
STARR
©1998 PITTSBURGH POST-GAZETTE
ROGERS

The scandals strangling the Clinton presidency were the biggest show in town.
- January 29, 1998

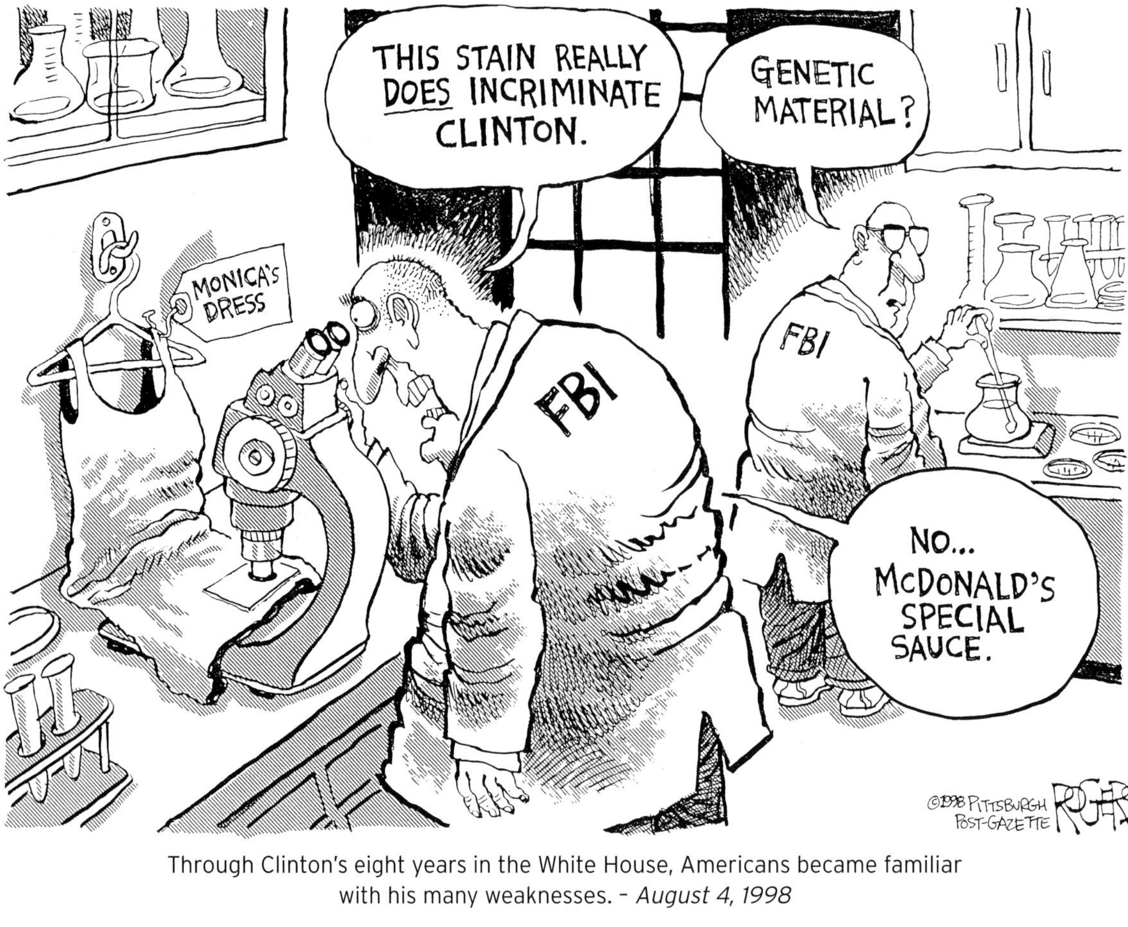
THIS STAIN REALLY DOES INCRIMINATE CLINTON.
GENETIC MATERIAL?
NO... McDONALD'S SPECIAL SAUCE.
MONICA'S DRESS
FBI
FBI
©1998 PITTSBURGH POST-GAZETTE
ROGERS

Through Clinton's eight years in the White House, Americans became familiar with his many weaknesses. *- August 4, 1998*

On many fronts the new Bush wanted to take the country back to a familiar time.
- *March 25, 2001*

On the first anniversary of 9/11, George W. Bush was obsessed with Iraq, not finding the mastermind of the attack on America. - *September 17, 2002*

When Bush ordered the invasion of Iraq, many Americans felt it was to free something besides the Iraqis. - *March 22, 2003*

Bush's basis for the Iraq war, Saddam Hussein's "weapons of mass destruction," never materialized. - *January 31, 2004*

Photos of Iraqis being tortured by U.S. soldiers at Abu Ghraib undercut
Americans' support for the war. - *May 9, 2004*

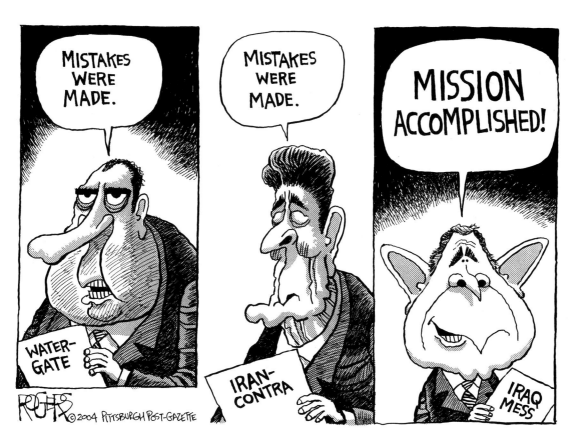

As the Iraq war dragged on, Bush refused to concede error.
- *October 12, 2004*

Vice President Dick Cheney accidentally shot a friend in the face while hunting quail in Texas.
- *February 14, 2006*

Even after leaving office, Dick Cheney defended the CIA's use of torture
while questioning Al-Qaeda suspects. - *December 12, 2014*

During the 2008 campaign, Barack Obama was criticized by the far right
for not wearing a flag lapel pin. - *July 8, 2008*

With the economy reeling, Americans were eager for the new president
to deliver his much-promised hope and change. - *January 25, 2009*

Barack Obama wanted a working relationship right off the bat with Congress, but Republicans weren't interested. – *February 13, 2009*

To get the economy going, Obama engineered a bailout for the failing auto industry. – *June 5, 2009*

In the 2010 congressional elections, Obama's Democratic Party lost control of the House and six seats in the Senate. - *November 9, 2010*

Almost 10 years after 9/11, the U.S. finally captured and killed Osama bin Laden, but the president's critics were unimpressed. - *May 3, 2011*

With Republicans seizing on the flaws of the Affordable Care Act, many Democrats faced a stiff test for re-election. – *March 21, 2014*

Normally a friend to environmentalists, the president broke ranks and proposed opening the Atlantic Ocean to drilling. – *February 3, 2015*

Dennis Roddy, June 9, 2018

Rob's politics and mine are not the same.

In fact, when I worked in Pennsylvania Governor Corbett's administration, he did his darnedest to make me unemployed. God knows I've wanted to choke Rob on more than one occasion. He's opinionated, unrestrained and a wisenheimer of the top chop. In short, he's doing his job. He is the indispensable irritant that keeps us scratching and thinking.

So, when Keith Burris, the newly installed opinion editor, arrived from out of town and started killing Rob's cartoons, we began to shudder a little. We've heard all sorts of explanations emanating from the building on Pittsburgh's North Shore: He's too harsh. He's too fixated on Donald Trump.

Then came the explanation that tipped us all off to how broken the place has become: that an editorial cartoonist is supposed to mirror the political positions of the newspaper and its publisher.

It's not true. In fact, it flies in the face of what a political cartoonist is supposed to do. Editorial cartoonists are the in-house dissenters, the newspaper equivalent of a small boy, snowball in hand, who spots a top hat passing on the other side of the fence and just can't resist.

Newspapers are more than private property. They are community institutions – civic trusts protected by the Constitution and, as such, part of a social contract. Their obligation is not only to be independent voices, but to elevate the culture by enabling and nurturing independence of thought.

That's what is so sad about the *Post-Gazette*'s attempt to turn its editorial cartoonist into an extension of a publisher's whims rather than a celebration of open debate and spirited dissent. All it takes is for one mediocre man or woman to place their comfort above the common good for a civic institution to run aground.

That's why editorial page editors should not be sycophants. Still, if Keith Burris chooses to be one, he should not expect others to follow. Even in this age of dissipating spirits, some of us still have souls. Rob Rogers is one of them. And today, he is more necessary than ever.

Dennis Roddy is an award-winning political consultant from Pittsburgh. He is a former columnist and reporter for the *Pittsburgh Post-Gazette* and former Special Assistant to Pennsylvania Governor Tom Corbett. This is an excerpt from an article originally written for **Pennlive.com**.

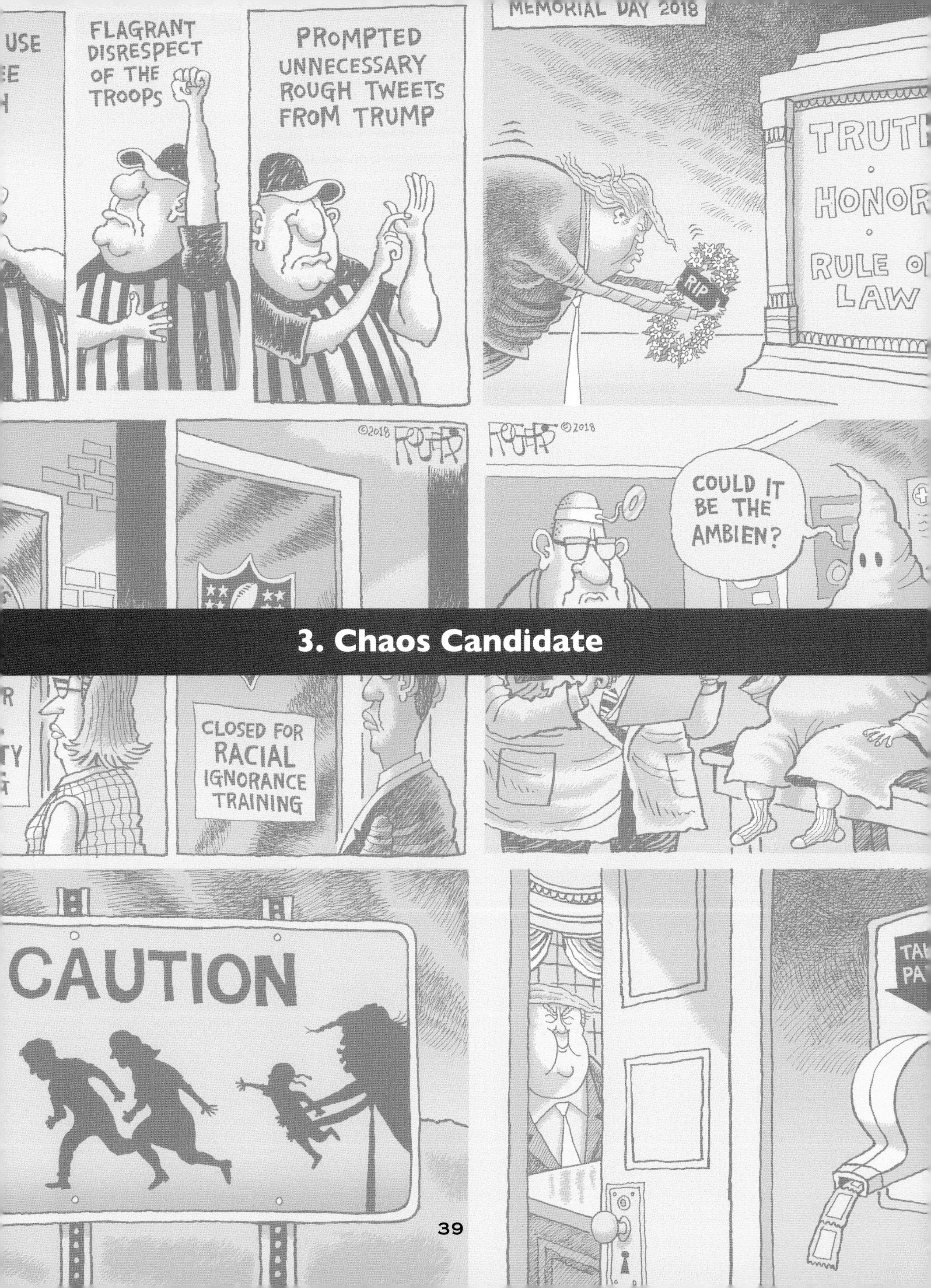
FLAGRANT DISRESPECT OF THE TROOPS
PROMPTED UNNECESSARY ROUGH TWEETS FROM TRUMP
MEMORIAL DAY 2018
RIP
TRUTH
HONOR
RULE OF LAW
©2018 ROGERS
ROGERS ©2018
COULD IT BE THE AMBIEN?
CLOSED FOR RACIAL IGNORANCE TRAINING
CAUTION

3. Chaos Candidate

Donald Trump has been on the world stage for decades as evidenced by my 1988 *Pittsburgh Press* cartoon that begins this chapter. He toyed with the idea of running for president before, most seriously in 2012. The campaign trail, with its rallies and press junkets, seemed tailored for Trump. He thrived on the reality show atmosphere and pro-wrestling theatrics. Of course, the Democrats (and other Republicans, for that matter) had their own reality show playing out, too. I have included some glimpses into their side of the campaign circus in this chapter.

My caricature of Trump may have changed over the years, but Trump's need to be the center of attention has not. It became clear from the moment he descended the golden escalator at Trump Tower in 2015 that this was not a mission to "Make America Great Again" - this was an ego trip for The Donald.

Trump's name was on just about everything in the '80s.
- *October 14, 1988*

My caricature of reality star Trump still needed some refinement.
- *February 16, 2004*

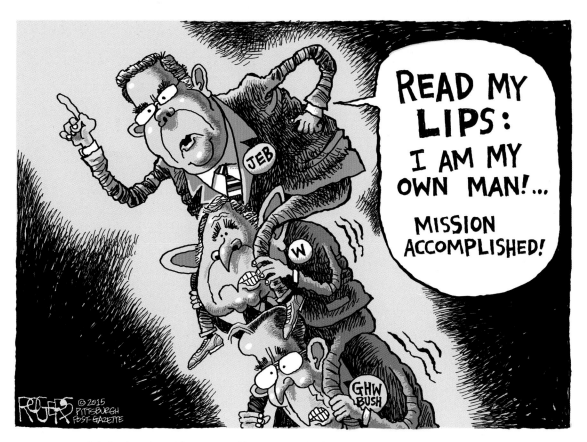

Jeb Bush entered the race as his own man, but couldn't escape the family legacy.
- February 26, 2015

Ted Cruz made his intentions known early.
- March 26, 2015

Meanwhile, the Democrats had all but crowned their candidate.
- April 14, 2015

Hillary debuted a logo that was new. The GOP responded with something old.
- April 23, 2015

Bernie Sanders energized the far left.
- May 3, 2015

Brother George's decision to go to war with Iraq became a sticking point for Jeb.
- May 14, 2015

Trump shocked the field when he announced his candidacy.
- *June 18, 2015*

Not all Democrats were enthralled by the idea of another Clinton White House.
- *August 20, 2015*

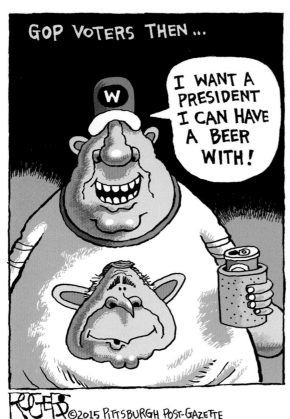

I WANT A PRESIDENT I CAN HAVE A BEER WITH!

I WANT A PRESIDENT I CAN SHARE HATEFUL RACIST, SEXIST AND XENOPHOBIC SLURS WITH!

©2015 PITTSBURGH POST-GAZETTE

Surprisingly, many conservative voters embraced the non-traditional Republican candidate.
- *September 15, 2015*

IF RONALD REAGAN WERE RUNNING TODAY...

©2015 PITTSBURGH POST-GAZETTE

YOU RAISED TAXES, MADE DEALS WITH OUR ENEMIES AND HAVE BEEN SOFT ON IMMIGRATION... LOOK AT THAT FACE!...WHO WOULD VOTE FOR THAT?

THERE YOU GO AGAIN!

The GOP candidates tried to out-Reagan each other, though none of them truly embraced his ideals.
- *September 17, 2015*

By Thanksgiving, there seemed to be no limit to the heights Trump's lies could soar.
- *November 26, 2015*

Not even the hype over the latest *Star Wars* movie *The Force Awakens* could
distract Americans from the campaign. - *December 6, 2015*

Did voters really believe in a xenophobic Santa Claus?
- *December 22, 2015*

Trump began to talk as though the law did not apply to him.
- *January 31, 2016*

The other GOP candidates struggled to be noticed amid the Trump media frenzy.
- *February 4, 2016*

A face only a leftist could love.
- *February 11, 2016*

Trump was leading the race by using only his own money, something that
confounded establishment donors. - *February 24, 2016*

Even in the primaries, Trump fanned the flames of Hillary's email problems.
- *March 13, 2016*

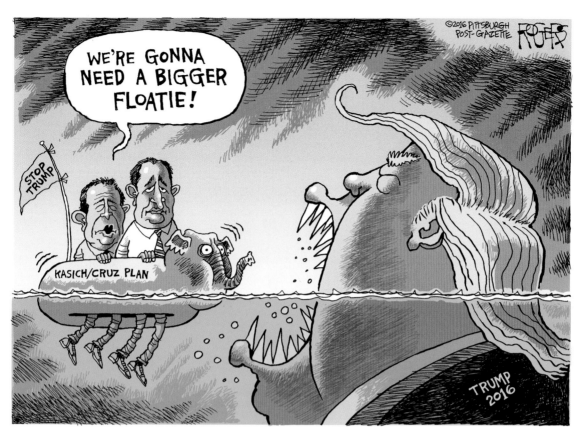

John Kasich and Ted Cruz plotted to deny Trump his delegates, but the ploy deflated quickly.
- *April 28, 2016*

After fierce debates and bloody primaries, Trump had the nomination in hand
before the convention. - *May 6, 2016*

Trump went out of his way to kiss up to the National Rifle Association.
- May 24, 2016

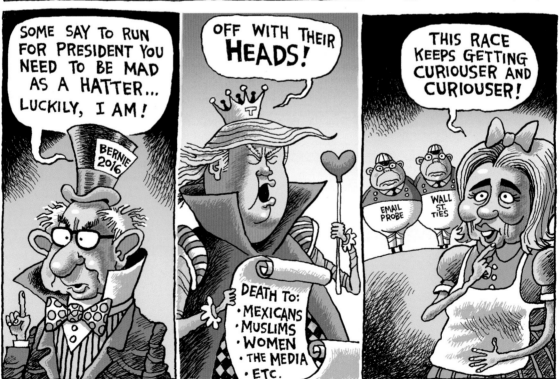

The new movie *Alice Through the Looking Glass* provided the perfect campaign metaphor.
- June 5, 2016

Hillary clinched the Democratic nomination, but Bernie refused to concede.
- *June 9, 2016*

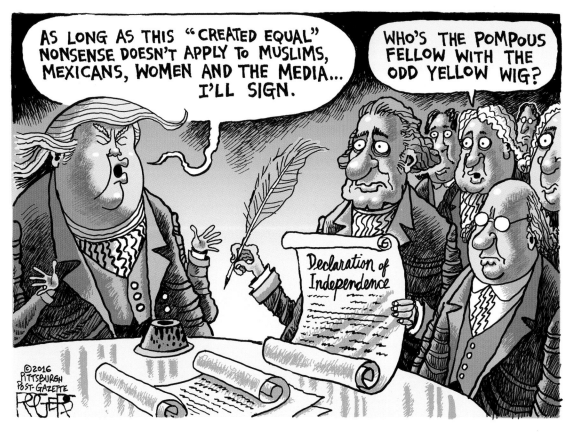

Under Trump, it appeared Independence Day would never be the same.
- *July 3, 2016*

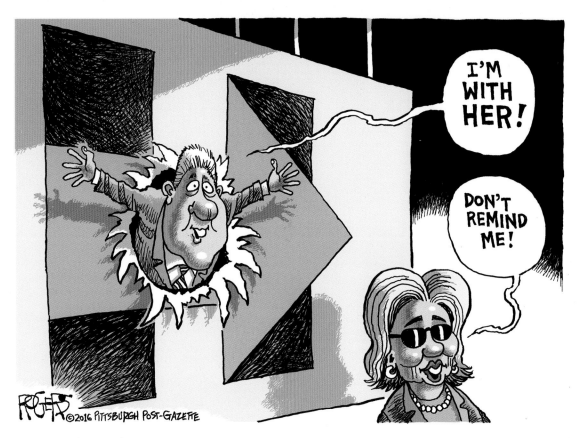

For better or worse, Bill began campaigning with Hillary.
- July 5, 2016

In past election years, my newspaper sent me to cover both the Republican and Democratic National Conventions. It was the one chance I had to step away from my drawing table and do some on-the-ground comics journalism and satire. I sent back daily sketchbooks of my observations along with a few fully finished editorial cartoons. It was always a lot of work, but it was a blast.

In 2016, management at my paper said they did not have enough in the budget to send me to cover the conventions. Thankfully, my friend Matt Bors at the The Nib was looking for someone with press credentials to cover the RNC in Cleveland. They were willing to pay enough to cover all of my costs and then some. I was in! I drew five six-panel comics, one for each of the four days of the convention, plus an intro cartoon to kick things off. Cleveland went so well, they paid me to do three more for the DNC in Philadelphia.

Here are my comics covering the 2016 political conventions.

AS A PITTSBURGH-BASED CARTOONIST, I'VE DRAWN MY SHARE OF CARTOONS ABOUT **CLEVELAND**...

CLEVELAND SUCKS!

STEELERS

BOTH CITIES LOVE THEIR SPORTS TEAMS...

LOOK... IT'S ELIZABETH WARREN!

BUT THIS WEEK I'LL BE COVERING A DIFFERENT KIND OF SPORT...

YOUR SHIRT IS BROWN TOO!

YA!

BROWNS

AS I DROVE INTO THE CITY, THE FIRST THING I SAW WAS A SIGN ATTACHED TO A PLANE... (YES, IT REALLY SAID THAT!)

HILLARY FOR PRISON 2016

CAN YOU RUN THE COUNTRY FROM JAIL?

THE BLACK STEEL PERIMETER FENCING MADE IT CLEAR THEY WERE TAKING SECURITY QUITE SERIOUSLY...

BUT I'M NOT MEXICAN!

NO ENTRY

THE **RNC** EVEN ASKED THE PUBLIC TO HELP IDENTIFY ANY SUSPICIOUS CHARACTERS...

IF YOU **SEE** SOMETHING, **SAY** SOMETHING!

THAT'S RIGHT... THE BUMPER STICKER SAYS "TRUMP FOR PRESIDENT."

ROB ROGERS © 2016 THE NIB

7/18/16

CLEVELAND KICKED OFF RNC WEEK WITH A BIG PARTY AT THE **ROCK** AND **ROLL HALL** OF **FAME**...

'CAUSE WHEN YOU THINK "GOP"... YOU THINK "ROCK AND ROLL"... RIGHT?

I HOPE THEY HAVE A LOT OF PAT BOONE STUFF!

I BOARDED A SHUTTLE TO THE PARTY NOT REALIZING IT WAS FULL OF **GOP** DELEGATES...

THE LAME-STREAM MEDIA IS TRYING TO MAKE US LOOK BAD!

GOOD THING I BROUGHT MY GUN!

TRUMP

THERE WERE THOUSANDS OF **GOP** DELEGATES AND GUESTS PACKED INTO THE NORTH COAST HARBOR GROUNDS... NO SURPRISE, THEY WERE 99% WHITE...

WOW... A PERSON OF COLOR!... TRUMP FAN?

NO... CATERER.

THE DELEGATES FELL INTO THREE BASIC CATEGORIES: ENTHUSIASTS, APOLOGISTS AND FATALISTS...

I LOVE TRUMP AS MUCH AS MY 13 CATS!

AT LEAST HE'S NOT CROOKED HILLARY!

WE'RE **DOOMED!**

THREE DOG NIGHT* PLAYED FOR THE DELEGATES...

♫ JEREMIAH WAS A BULLFROG... ♫

SO IS **HILLARY!**

* YEP... MORE OLD WHITE GUYS!

AS THE **SUN** SET OVER **LAKE ERIE**... I BEGAN TO HAVE A BETTER SENSE OF WHAT MADE THESE PEOPLE TICK...

THE SUN IS GOING DOWN.

IT'S ALL OBAMA'S FAULT.

ROB ROGERS © 2016 THE NIB

7/19/16

NAVIGATING THE GAUNTLET OF **SECURITY** CHECKS AND CREDENTIAL SNAFUS WAS TOUGH... BUT I FINALLY MADE IT INSIDE **QUICKEN** LOAN CENTER

WHICH WAY TO THE CARTOONISTS' SUITE?

?

SECURITY

THE **RNC** WAS EMPHASIZING "**UNITY**" AS DELEGATES TUSSLED...

UNBIND THE DELEGATES... AND MY NECK!

NO!

DESPITE **TRUMP'S** PROMISE OF A FANTASTIC SHOW... THE SPEAKERS LIST LEFT A LOT TO BE DESIRED...

YOU MAY REMEMBER ME FROM "HAPPY DAYS."

POTSIE'S A REPUBLICAN?

WHAT HAPPENS WHEN **DONALD** RUNS OUT OF FAMILY MEMBERS?... WHO'S NEXT... THE SERVANTS?

I'M TRUMP'S BARBER... BOY, THE STORIES I COULD TELL...

BUT I SIGNED A NON-DISCLOSURE AGREEMENT.

THE DOG-WHISTLE NARRATIVE WAS A LITTLE DISTURBING...

WOOF

BLUE LIVES MATTER... NO BLACK AMERICA... MAKE AMERICA SAFE AGAIN...

WOOF

WOOF

WOOF

TEXAS

IOWA

OHIO

PERSONALLY, I'D LIKE TO SEE THEM GIVE **MELANIA** A **DO-OVER**...

ASK NOT WHAT DONALD CAN DO FOR YOU...

MAKE AMERICA PLAGIARIZE AGAIN

ROB ROGERS © 2016 THE NIB

7/20/16

THE **MEDIA** PRESENCE IS INSANE... BY MY COUNT THERE ARE **1,379** JOURNALISTS FOR EVERY DELEGATE...

WHO ARE YOU WEARING?

THE **PROTESTERS** WERE ALSO OUTNUMBERED...

TRASH TRUMP

WHO ARE YOU WEARING?

THERE ARE SEVERAL **LEVELS** OF MEDIA CREDENTIALS TO HELP YOU CONTEMPLATE YOUR SELF WORTH...

FULL ACCESS — I'M THE **BEST!**

GENERAL — I'M OK...

PERIMETER — I AM GARBAGE... DON'T LOOK AT ME

WHEN I SNAGGED A **FLOOR** PASS I FELT LIKE THE KID WHO FOUND A **GOLDEN** TICKET IN WILLY WONKA...

♪ WHO CAN TAKE THE SUNSHINE... SPRINKLE IT WITH DEW? ♫

TRUMP, OF COURSE!

ONCE ON THE CONVENTION **FLOOR,** I BEGAN MY SEARCH FOR **VIPs**...

YOU LOOK FAMILIAR... ARE YOU SOMEBODY?... WHAT ABOUT HIM?... IS HE?

I SPOTTED **ONE** PROMINENT REPUBLICAN WHO DECIDED **NOT** TO STAY HOME... HE LOOKED STUNNED.

OFF WITH HER HEAD!... OFF WITH HER HEAD!

THIS IS <u>NOT</u> BOB DOLE'S REPUBLICAN PARTY!

KANSAS

ROB ROGERS © 2016 THE NIB

7/21/16

THE **RNC** IS SUPPOSED TO HELP THE PARTY FALL IN LOVE WITH THEIR CHOSEN **NOMINEE**...

NO TONGUE!

BUT REPUBLICANS SEEM MORE INTERESTED IN **HATING** HILLARY THAN IN **LOVING** DONALD...

WHERE'S YOUR TRUMP BUTTON?

JAIL HILLARY

CROOKED HILLARY!

KICK HILLARY

HELL NO

RATS...I KNEW I FORGOT SOMETHING!

THE **VITRIOLIC SPEECHES** DIDN'T HELP REDIRECT THE PASSION...

HILLARY'S WORSE THAN 9-11!

RUDY

IT DOESN'T TAKE A BRAIN SURGEON TO SEE HILLARY IS THE DEVIL!

BEN

CHRIS **CHRISTIE** TURNED IT INTO A **BLOOD SPORT**...

GUILTY?

HILLARY'S ONLY **REPRIEVE** WAS WHEN THE CROWD TURNED ON **CRUZ**...

VOTE YOUR CONSCIENCE!

OUR CONSCIENCE TELLS US TO DISEMBOWEL YOU!

IN THE END, **TRUMP** CONTINUED DOWN THE DARK, SCARY PATH...

THE FOUR HORSEMEN OF OUR CURRENT **APOCALYPSE** ARE HILLARY, HILLARY HILLARY AND HILLARY!

ROB ROGERS © 2016 THE NIB

7/22/16

AFTER A LONG WEEK COVERING THE **RNC** IN **CLEVELAND** I WAS HAVING TROUBLE TRANSITIONING...

HER HAIR ISN'T RIGHT!

THE **DEMS** ARE HERE IN PHILLY TO NOMINATE **HILLARY**... BUT I WAS STILL SEEING A LOT OF **LOVE** FOR SANDERS...

I LOVE HIM!

SOME DEMS ARE **NOT** HAPPY WITH THE CHOICE OF **TIM KAINE** FOR **VP**... THEY WERE HOPING FOR A MORE "PROGRESSIVE" CHOICE

THIS "NAME YOUR PRICE" TOOL CAN BE USED FOR HEALTH CARE, COLLEGE TUITION, EQUAL PAY, ETC.

PROGRESSIVE

FLO FOR VP

BUT THE REAL PROBLEM THIS WEEK SEEMS TO BE THE HEAT...

DO YOU SMELL THAT?

YES... IT SMELLS LIKE A TRUMP PRESIDENCY!

DNC EMAILS

DEBBIE WASSERMAN SCHULTZ WAS THE CONVENTION'S FIRST CASUALTY...

THE "**UNITY BELL**" DEFINITELY HAS A CRACK IN IT...

LET CHAOS RING!

HILLARY

7/26/16

ROB ROGERS © 2016

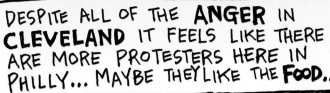

DESPITE ALL OF THE **ANGER** IN **CLEVELAND** IT FEELS LIKE THERE ARE MORE PROTESTERS HERE IN PHILLY... MAYBE THEY LIKE THE **FOOD**...

MMM... THIS CHEESESTEAK ALMOST MAKES ME FORGET THE OPPRESSIVE OVERLORDS RUNNING FOR PRESIDENT...

THEY WERE PROTESTING EVERYTHING FROM THE **SERIOUS** TO THE **SILLY**...

BLACK LIVES MATTER

WOMEN'S LIVES MATTER

ANIMAL LIVES MATTER

BATTERY LIVES MATTER

MY CELL WON'T HOLD A CHARGE!

THERE WAS EVEN A NONPARTISAN RALLY FOCUSED ON MENTAL ILLNESS...

NONPARTISAN... SO YOU THINK <u>ALL</u> THE CANDIDATES ARE CRAZY?... I AGREE!

NOT EXACTLY.

LESS JAIL, MORE TREATMENT

OUTSIDE THE WELLS FARGO CENTER THE "**BERNIE** OR **BUST**" CROWD GREW...

HELL, NO, DNC... WE WON'T VOTE FOR HILLARY!

WON'T THAT HELP TRUMP?

LOGIC AND ANARCHY DON'T MIX!

INSIDE THE **HALL**, DIVISIVE RANCOR GAVE WAY TO CELEBRATION AS DELEGATES MADE HISTORY BY NOMINATING THE **FIRST WOMAN**

I WAS THE FIRST **MAN**... DOESN'T THAT COUNT FOR ANYTHING?

NOT THIS YEAR!

BILL CLINTON SEEMED A LITTLE UNCOMFORTABLE IN THE ROLE OF SUPPORTIVE SPOUSE...

HILLARY'S NO QUITTER...

SHE STUCK WITH <u>THIS</u> OLD HOUND DOG!

7/28/16

ROB ROGERS © 2016

THE **DNC** WAS MARKED BY **OUTREACH** TO BLACKS, WOMEN, **LGBT**, MUSLIMS, LATINOS AND THE DISABLED...

WE ARE THE PARTY OF INCLUSION!

I FEEL LEFT OUT!

THEIR MESSAGE OF OPTIMISM WAS IN STARK CONTRAST TO THE **GLOOM** AND **DOOM** OF THE **RNC**...

I'M GONNA SUE THEM FOR USING MY NAME!

LOVE TRUMPS HATE

LOVE TRUMPS HATE

LOVE TRUM HATE

EVEN **BERNIE SANDERS** HOPPED ON BOARD THE **HILLARY** BUS...

I'M HAPPY TO SUPPORT HILLARY... THIS IS MY HAPPY FACE!

THOUGH NOT **ALL** OF HIS SUPPORTERS WERE ABLE TO SAY THE **WORDS**...

I SUPPORT BERNILLARY... ER... I MEAN... I'M WITH HERNIE... I MEAN...

Bernie 2016

HILLARY REBUKED **TRUMP'S** CLAIM THAT HE **ALONE** COULD FIX AMERICA...

IT TAKES A VILLAGE... NOT A VILLAGE IDIOT!

WHETHER VOTERS SEE HER AS A GROUND-BREAKING **CHANGE-MAKER** OR A POLARIZING FIGURE, THERE IS NO DENYING THE **HISTORY** SHE IS MAKING...

SO LONG, **PHILLY**... HELLO, FIGHT OF THE **CENTURY!**

YO, HILLARY!

7/31/16

ROB ROGERS © 2016

Trump's acceptance speech at the Republican National Convention was like no other.
- *July 24, 2016*

As if Hillary didn't have enough email troubles, WikiLeaks released thousands of embarrassing emails on the eve of the Democratic convention. - *July 25, 2016*

Trump was brazen enough to go to war with a Gold Star family.
- August 3, 2016

THE 2016 TRUMP OLYMPICS...

The Summer Olympics in Rio de Janeiro were no match for the 2016 Trump Games.
- August 5, 2016

Trump's effusive praise for Vladimir Putin stunned GOP leaders.
- *August 9, 2016*

The Republican nominee continued to shock the world with racist and xenophobic proposals.
- *August 30, 2016*

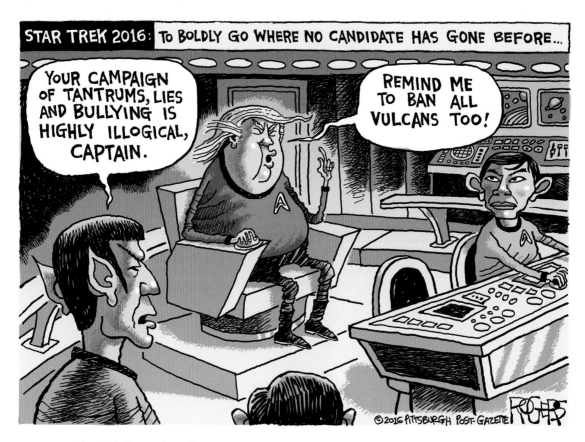

Star Trek: Beyond, another summer movie, provided fodder for at least one cartoonist.
- September 9, 2016

Trump creepily stalked Clinton on the debate stage in St. Louis.
- October 11, 2016

WHAT KIND OF LOCKER ROOM IS TRUMP HANGING OUT IN?

ASSAULT — GROPING — SEXISM — MISOGYNY — TRUMP

The "Access Hollywood" tape in which Trump bragged about sexually assaulting women
was dismissed by his campaign as locker-room talk. – *October 14, 2016*

A CHOICE BETWEEN "FIRSTS"...

©2016 PITTSBURGH POST-GAZETTE

THE FIRST WALL-BUILDING, MUSLIM-BANNING, HANDICAP-MOCKING, GOLD STAR FAMILY-TRASHING, GENITAL-GRABBING, ANGRY-TWEETING, ORANGE-FACED REALITY SHOW BULLY...

OR...

IT'S RIGGED!

THE FIRST WOMAN

On the eve of the election, voters weighed a choice between two historic firsts.
– *November 7, 2016*

Although the election results didn't come in until after my deadline, this post-election cartoon was suitable for either outcome. – *November 8, 2016*

Breitbart's Steve Bannon and other hate-group forces in the alt-right movement had found a champion in President-elect Trump. – *November 15, 2016*

In a repeat of 2000, the popular-vote winner did not become president. Why do we still elect people this way? – *November 27, 2016*

It soon became clear that America's next president had little understanding of the Constitution. – *December 1, 2016*

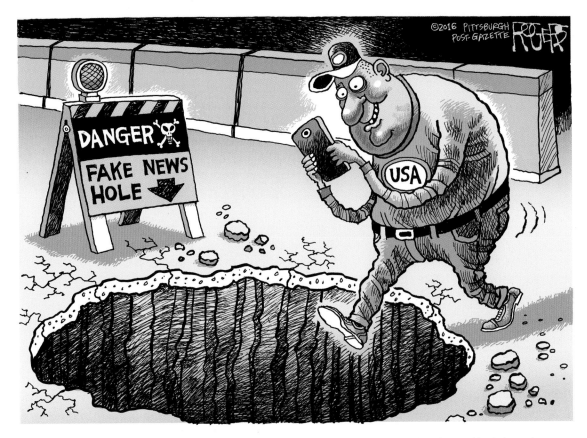

Prodded by Trump, some Americans bought into lies and conspiracy theories on the Internet as long as they reinforced their own beliefs. - *December 9, 2016*

TRUMP'S LATEST CABINET PICKS...

Trump claimed he was choosing all the best people for his Cabinet, but the opposite appeared to be true. - *December 19, 2016*

Given Trump's ego and narcissism, the New Year did not seem to bode well for planet Earth.
- December 30, 2016

Steve Brodner, June 5, 2018

This is a story of the slow bleeding to near death of one of the great editorial cartoon careers in the country and also, more broadly, the loss of decency in positions of power as the Trump Effect gives people everywhere license to exhibit long-held authoritarian, nationalist and racist tendencies.

Rob Rogers, editorial cartoonist for the *Pittsburgh Post-Gazette*, is one of the best in the world. His gifts are very special. I have called him the Venus flytrap of cartooning because his toons are immediately entertaining and then, on further inspection, reveal insight and power. He has won just about all the awards the field has to offer. And, as it happens, is as decent and honest a person as you will find.

For the last quarter-century Rob's publisher, John Robinson Block, a wealthy man from a publishing family which also owns the *Toledo Blade*, has had a respectful hands-off approach to Rob's work. Since the election of Donald Trump that all changed. Block has changed. With the currents of anti-immigrationism, attacks on the Constitution, media, courts and apologies for racism, people everywhere, and Mr. Block in particular, have become emboldened, like the Republican Party, to walk and talk like Trump. Not long ago Block hired editor Keith Burris, whose achievements include a widely derided editorial defending Trump's "shithole" defamation of Haiti and other needy and developing countries. This would be the man now overseeing the work of Rob Rogers. You can pretty much write the rest.

I don't know what Rob's options are at this point. One would doubt the capacity of these trends to turn themselves around. But it is, to me, the job of the graphic arts, media community, and the nation at large to raise its voice as one in protest. Freedom of speech is established for cartoonists and columnists as a given. They are not subject to fashion. The right of artists and writers to remain free, especially in times of constitutional crisis must be inviolate. The absolute worst thing now would be silence surrounding the silencing of Rob Rogers.

Please share his work and his story. And give 'em hell.

Steve Brodner is an independent illustrator, caricaturist, journalist and educator. His work has appeared in most major publications in the United States. This originally appeared on Brodner's Facebook page.

4. A Day in the Life of a Cartoonist

L et's take a brief break from all of this talk about being fired and explore the editorial cartoonist's creative process. Do you think surgeons are ever asked, "What kind of scalpel do you use?" As a cartoonist, I get asked that all the time. Not about scalpels, but about what kind of pen I use. I guess it's because everybody can relate to drawing pictures. We all draw as kids. It's something everyone has tried at least once. You can't really say the same thing about open-heart surgery.

But it's not just about the pen. Today's cartoonists work on computers with Photoshop or other graphic software. They draw on screens or tablets with a stylus. Some even do their entire cartoons on iPads. It's a brave new world.

I still prefer ink on paper but I do all of my color and finish work on the computer. Here is some of what's involved in creating an editorial cartoon.

WHAT DOES IT TAKE TO CREATE AN EDITORIAL CARTOON?

BY ROB ROGERS ©2016

LET ME DRAW YOU A PICTURE!

STEP 1: FIND A TOPIC THAT BEGS FOR SATIRE...

NEWS

GOP CANDIDATES COMPARE PENIS SIZE

HELLO?

STEP 2: CHOOSE THE PERFECT METAPHOR...

I CAN'T DRAW GENITALS IN A FAMILY NEWSPAPER... BUT HANDS ARE OK...

THINGS WITH SMALL HANDS: BABY WATCH T-REX

STEP 3: CREATE A ROUGH SKETCH USING YOUR FAVORITE SKETCHING TOOL...

TRUMPZILLA

SOME CARTOONISTS SKETCH WITH A PEN...

SOME USE A PENCIL

AND SOME USE A TABLET.

MAGIC *Etch A Sketch*

STEP 4: TRANSFER THE SKETCH USING A LIGHT TABLE OR SOME OTHER BLACK MAGIC...

STEP 5: INK THE CARTOON USING YOUR INKING TOOL OF CHOICE...

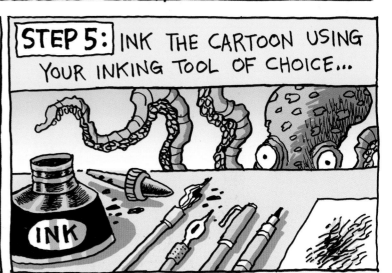

INK

STEP 6: ADD COLOR...

BY HAND...

TRUMPZILLA

OR DIGITALLY... WHY ISN'T THIS WORKING?

STEP 7: STAND BACK AND WATCH AS READERS REACT TO YOUR BRILLIANCE...

I DON'T GET IT.

GIVE IT A SEC...

NEWS

I STILL DON'T GET IT.

GIVE IT ANOTHER SEC...

I DON'T HAVE ALL DAY!

TRUMPZILLA

MY SMALL HANDS DON'T SEEM TO BE SLOWING ME DOWN AT ALL!

TRUMPZILLA

MY SMALL HANDS DON'T SEEM TO BE SLOWING ME DOWN AT ALL!

This book focuses on my cartoons about Donald Trump, the forty-fifth president of the United States, but as a political cartoonist I cover a lot of other important topics. Many of my cartoons deal with serious subjects – gun violence, women's rights, climate change and health care, to name a few. These are not funny topics and not all political cartoons are meant to be funny. But humor is a powerful tool. To me, the best political cartoons are those that can be provocative, hard-hitting and funny at the same time. Here is a sampling of some of the non-Trump cartoons I've drawn in recent years.

Small government sounds good to many Americans until something like Hurricane Irene hammers the East Coast. – *September 2, 2011*

Republican legislators pushed a bill in Virginia that required a woman to have a transvaginal ultrasound before receiving an abortion. – *March 2, 2012*

Republicans in many states resorted to gerrymandering and voter ID laws
to gain electoral advantage. – *June 8, 2012*

A World Bank report sounded a new warning about the dangers of climate change.
– *November 2, 2012*

Finally, the pope got his own Twitter account.
- *December 6, 2012*

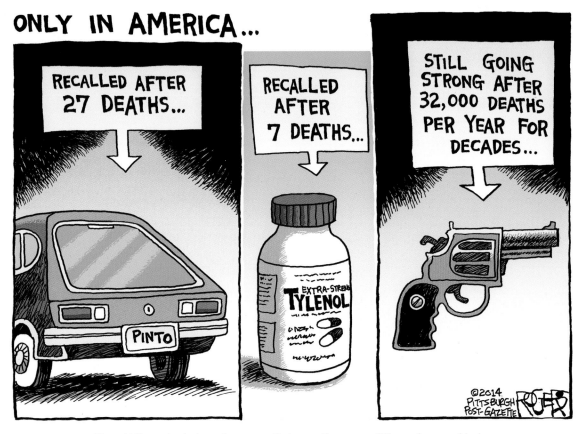

Many U.S. products have been recalled over the years. Others deserved to be.
- *June 3, 2014*

Multiple investigations revealed a pattern of negligence by the VA health system in treating military veterans. – *June 8, 2014*

Frustrated by an intransigent Congress that failed to pass immigration reform, President Barack Obama took executive action to block deportations. – *November 25, 2014*

Cartoonists of the world united in support of the victims of France's Charlie Hebdo massacre.
- *January 8, 2015*

War, violence and terror have been waged in the name of God for centuries.
- *January 13, 2015*

After white supremacist Dylann Roof murdered nine African Americans in a Charleston, S.C., church, it was clear that no place was safe from gun violence. - *August 30, 2015*

Europe's refugee crisis failed to nudge the United States to accept more migrants from Africa and the Middle East. - *November 19, 2015*

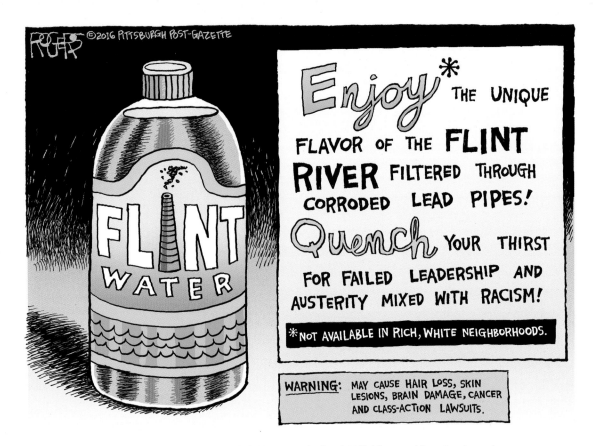

A government-appointed civil rights commission in Michigan said systemic racism helped to cause the Flint water crisis. – *January 20, 2016*

Mattel unveiled a new line of Barbie dolls that came in three body types and several skin tones. – *January 29, 2016*

POKÉMON GO MAKES EVERYTHING MORE FUN!

The video game Pokemon Go gave players a chance to battle and capture
virtual creatures in their real-world location. - *July 15, 2016*

Many Americans missed the point of black NFL players taking a knee
during the National Anthem. - *September 1, 2016*

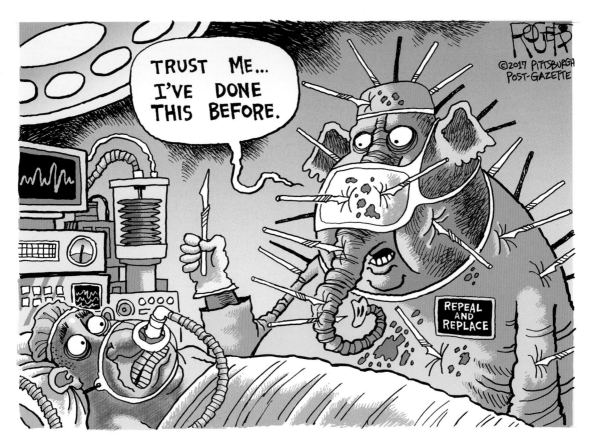

Congressional Republicans continued their never-ending quest
to repeal and replace Obamacare. – *September 22, 2017*

Sexual abuse and harassment claims in other industries made clear that
the #MeToo movement wasn't confined to Hollywood. – *October 22, 2017*

AS AMERICAN AS...

BASEBALL

APPLE PIE

MASS SHOOTINGS

AND FAILED LEADERSHIP

THOUGHTS AND PRAYERS...

GOP   I ♥ NRA

A 19-year-old gunman killed 17 students and staff at
Marjory Stoneman Douglas High School in Parkland, Fla. – *February 16, 2018*

©2018 ANDREWS McMEEL SYNDICATE

★★★★★★★
CELEBRATE
AMERICAN
INDEPENDENCE

↖ RED FIREWORKS

BLUE FIREWORKS ↗

America's new state of independence seems to mean independence from each other.
– *July 3, 2018*

Ann Telnaes, July 18, 2018

Cartoons are powerful.

Through satire and ridicule, humor and pointed caricatures, editorial cartoonists criticize leaders and governments who are behaving badly. Our purpose is to hold politicians and powerful institutions accountable to the people they are supposed to serve.

Cartoonists have been targeted throughout history by humorless politicians and heads of state. From Honoré Daumier being imprisoned for drawing the French king as Gargantua to Ali Ferzat's hands being broken over his critical cartoons of Syrian President Bashar al-Assad, cartoonists are jailed and physically attacked because, through their satire, they threaten those who are abusing their power. Even in countries with traditions of free expression, as we've experienced in Denmark and France, cartoonists have been threatened and killed by Islamic fundamentalists over cartoons they perceive offensive to their religious beliefs.

Why do cartoons cause such a visceral response? Because cartoons are universal, every human being responds to these seemingly simple drawings. They transcend language and class. Everyone, from the highly educated to the illiterate, the one-percenters to the average working person, can relate and see themselves in cartoons.

Here in the United States, editorial cartoonists have the protection of the First Amendment to ensure their voices are not silenced by the government or a thin-skinned president. But with the firing of longtime *Pittsburgh Post-Gazette* cartoonist Rob Rogers over cartoons critical of the president, we now see that censorship can be accomplished without an authoritarian president's orders. The danger today comes from the enablers and powerful supporters willing to quash dissent and undermine the institution of a free press for him.

Ann Telnaes is a Pulitzer Prize-winning editorial cartoonist and animator for *The Washington Post*. This piece was written for *Spiked: The Unpublished Political Cartoons of Rob Rogers*, an exhibition at George Washington University's Corcoran School of the Arts and Design.

5. Trump Year One: American Carnage

After Donald Trump became president, friends would come up to me at social events and say things like, "You must be loving this... the cartoons just draw themselves!" Not exactly. First, there is just too much material. If a cartoon topic is a drink of water, covering Trump is like trying to take a sip from a fire hydrant. It almost knocks you over with sheer volume. Plus, cartoonists depend on the tools of exaggeration and caricature to make a point. Trump is so much of a caricature already and his behavior so absurd, that it is difficult to exaggerate him in a compelling way.

That said, my best cartoons are created when I am addressing an issue that I feel passionate about. Trump is certainly the most bizarre and colorful president I have ever covered. It is impossible not to have strong feelings about him. People are either passionately for Trump, or passionately against him. There is no in between. He won't be ignored.

Here are a few sips from the hydrant.

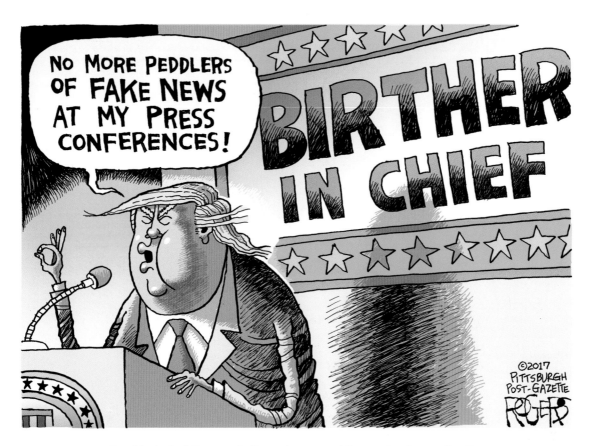

President-elect Trump, of all people, accused the media of spreading lies.
- *January 17, 2017*

Voters witnessed a swearing-in that led to much swearing across the United States.
- *January 20, 2017*

Trump's inaugural "American carnage" speech was historic if only for its bleakness.
- *January 24, 2017*

The president's hyper-nationalist anti-immigration rhetoric was red meat to his base.
- *January 31, 2017*

Soon after taking office, Trump made it clear that protecting
the family businesses was a priority. – *February 10, 2017*

The president was bothered more by White House leaks to the press than
his appearing to be a Russian agent. – *February 16, 2017*

Barely a month in office, Trump held his first presidential press conference.
It went as expected. – *February 19, 2017*

Soon to become a favorite Trump whipping boy, Attorney General nominee
Jeff Sessions kept faith with his future boss. – *March 3, 2017*

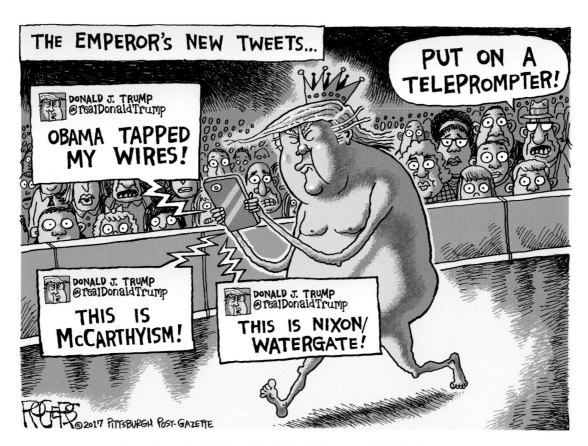

In another naked attempt to distract, Trump used Twitter to accuse
former President Barack Obama of wiretapping. – *March 7, 2017*

Who needs a White House communications director when there's Twitter?
– *March 23, 2017*

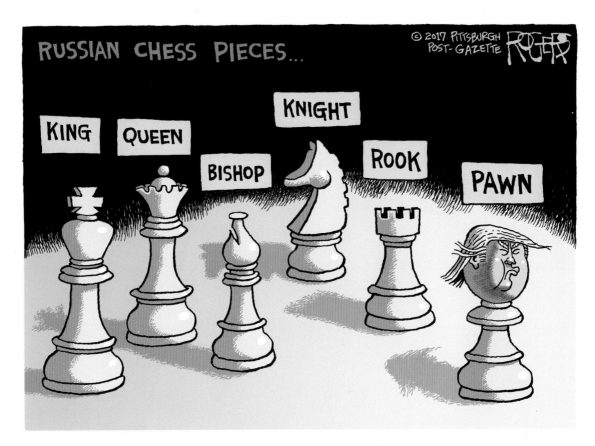

Intrigue mounted over the Russia connections to Trump's inner circle,
but one thing was becoming clear: This was not a game. - *March 26, 2017*

The feud between alt-right icon Steve Bannon and family confidantes
"Jarvanka" reached a fever pitch. - *April 16, 2017*

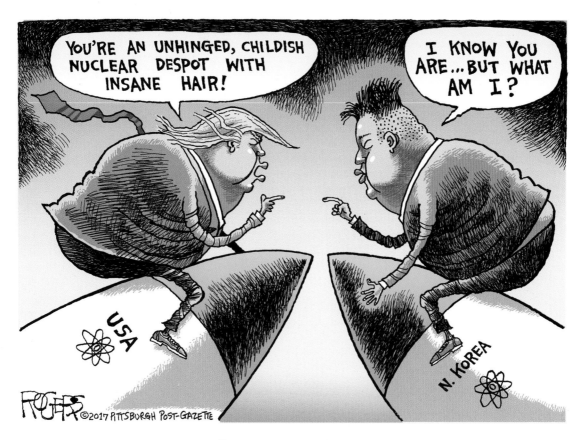

Name-calling helped Trump win the nomination.
No one expected it to become a tool of foreign policy. – *April 20, 2017*

While the world recoiled at the chemical attacks in Syria,
Trump was planning his own toxic releases. – *April 27, 2017*

President Nixon's "Saturday Night Massacre" had nothing on Donald Trump.
- May 11, 2017

It's hard to imagine the Mexicans paying for this one.
- May 18, 2017

The firing of Comey only fueled the Russia investigation, which Trump dubbed a "witch hunt."
– May 21, 2017

In announcing his withdrawal from the Paris climate accord,
Trump invoked an outdated notion of Pittsburgh. – June 5, 2017

Trump shared more qualities with Korean nemesis Kim Jong Un than first thought.
- *June 16, 2017*

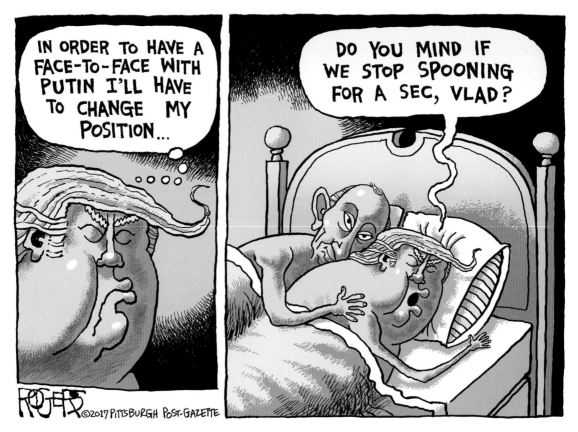

The president faced heat and suspicion from U.S. allies for seeking a private meeting
with Russia's Vladimir Putin at the G20 summit in Germany. - *July 7, 2017*

CANDIDATE JEKYLL and PRESIDENT HYDE...

Despite pledging support in his campaign for LGBTQ Americans,
it didn't take long for Trump to forget about them. - *July 28, 2017*

The president was so busy tearing down the previous administration
that he couldn't see his own disaster. - *August 1, 2017*

As scientists released their latest climate study,
Trump met the warning with his usual denials. – *August 11, 2017*

Violent protests by white nationalists killed one person and injured 19 in Charlottesville, Va.,
but a day later Trump condemned hate "on many sides." – *August 14, 2017*

Trump's soft spot for white nationalists and other hate groups became apparent
after Charlottesville. – *August 17, 2017*

While various states tore down statues honoring the Confederacy,
GOP leaders stood by Trump even in his racially charged rhetoric. – *August 18, 2017*

As Texas coped with a hurricane, Trump used a presidential pardon to rescue Joe Arpaio, the former Arizona sheriff convicted of using aggressive tactics against illegal immigrants. - *August 28, 2017*

Trump continued to frighten "Dreamers" with his anti-immigrant rhetoric and threats to tear up DACA.
- *September 7, 2017*

Battered and reviled as Trump's press secretary, Sean Spicer resigned and found a friendly spotlight two months later during a surprise walk-on at the Emmy Awards. – *September 19, 2017*

After some NFL players protested racism by kneeling during the National Anthem, Trump took a knee on the First Amendment. – *September 26, 2017*

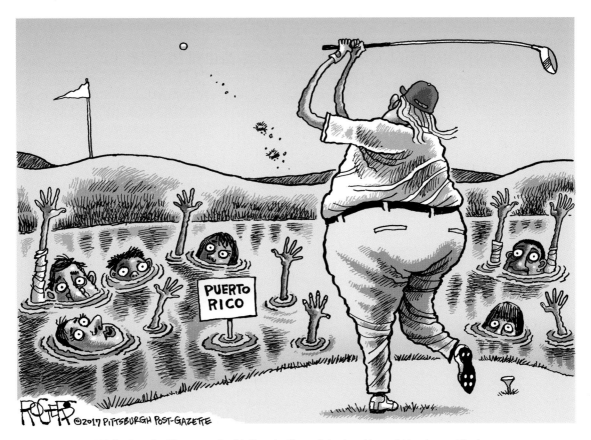

While Puerto Rico coped with the death and destruction of Hurricane Maria,
Trump logged his 67th day at a golf course as president. – *October 1, 2017*

Trashing Obama's achievements became Trump's renewable energy source.
– *October 13, 2017*

Trump allowed the release of classified JFK assassination files, posing the question, at least to a cartoonist, of whether the president thought Oswald had accomplices. – *October 26, 2017*

The president couldn't resist repeating his "Pocahontas" slur against Sen. Elizabeth Warren during a ceremony honoring Native American war heroes. – *November 30, 2017*

Roy Moore, accused of making sexual advances on teenage girls, was endorsed by Trump in the U.S. Senate race in Alabama. — *December 10, 2017*

With Trump still refusing to endorse U.S. intelligence agencies' view that Russians hacked the 2016 election, the White House revealed that he and Putin had spoken three times in the last six weeks. — *December 31, 2017*

Joel Pett, June 18, 2018

A cartoonist is jailed. Another is charged with treason. A cartoonist disappears. Another is threatened by government goons. Throngs march against a perceived cartoon's slight. That's how it goes for editorial cartoonists in Syria, Turkey, Iran, Malaysia and other troubled areas around the globe. But not here. In corporate America, cartoonists merely lose their livelihoods. I'm not comparing unemployment to incarceration, but with those livelihoods go the paychecks, the health care, the secure retirements, the legal protections and a lot more.

Strident, no-holds-barred newspaper editorial cartooning, spiraling into an inexorable death throe for at least two decades, bleaches into a pile of bones on a changing media landscape, all due to uncertain advertising economics, right?

But what if it's worse? What if losing our jobs is more than a lamentable byproduct of the well-documented industry convulsions that have also sidelined armies of shoe-leather reporters, photographers, copy editors, art critics, columnists and on and on?

What if editorial cartoonists were not just victims of economic hard times, but unabashedly discarded for challenging the country's leadership and direction? And what if this happened to mainstream cartoonists, at big-city dailies, during an administration which has expressed admiration for thug regimes around the globe and promoted policies akin to tinpot dictatorships?

It just happened to Rob Rogers at the *Pittsburgh Post-Gazette*.

Joel Pett is the Pulitzer Prize-winning editorial cartoonist for the *Lexington Herald-Leader* and board president of the Cartoonists Rights Network International. This was originally written for the CRNI web site.

6. You’re Killing Me

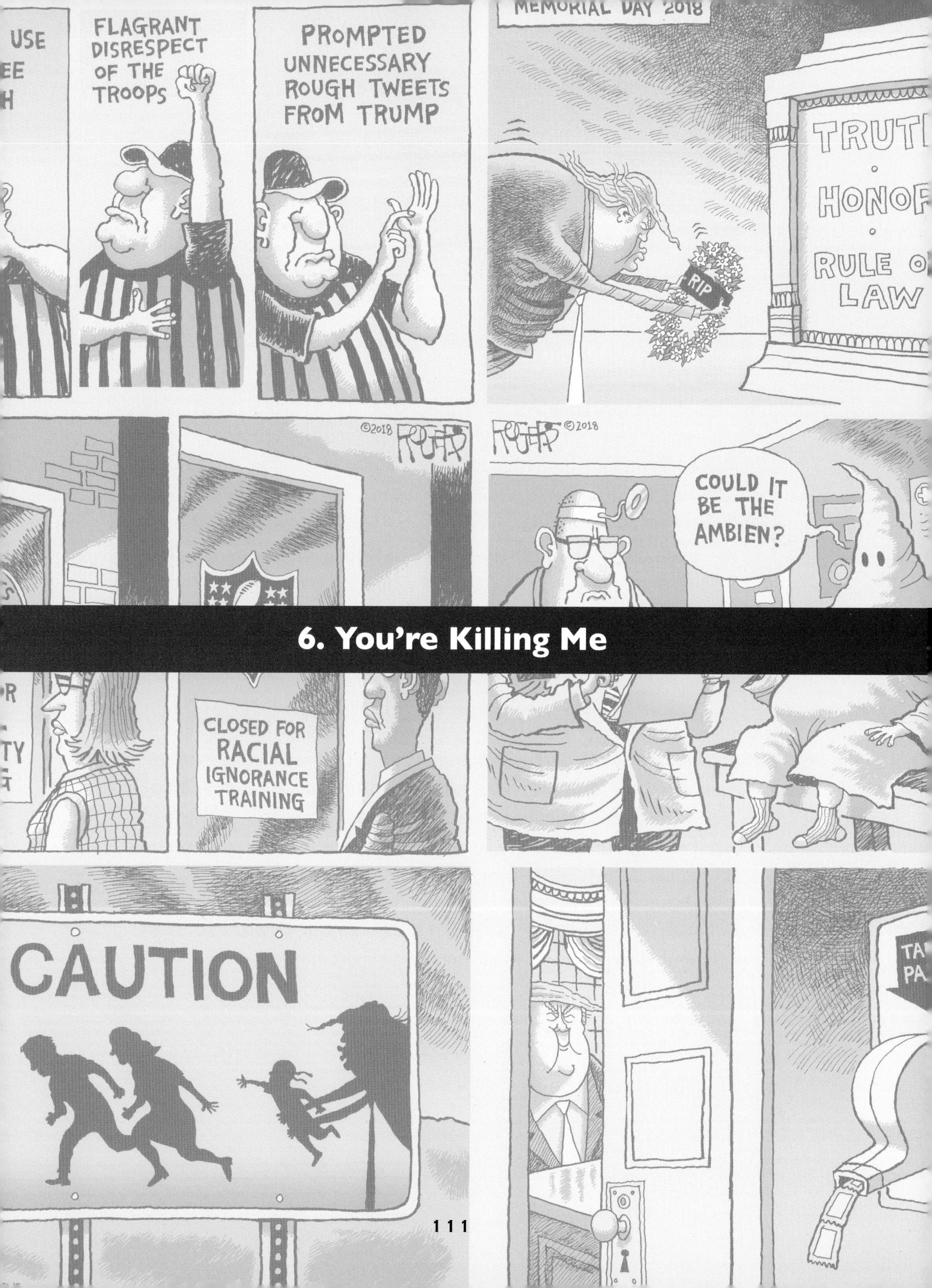
FLAGRANT DISRESPECT OF THE TROOPS
PROMPTED UNNECESSARY ROUGH TWEETS FROM TRUMP
MEMORIAL DAY 2018
RIP
TRUTH
HONOR
RULE OF LAW
©2018 ROGERS
CLOSED FOR RACIAL IGNORANCE TRAINING
COULD IT BE THE AMBIEN?
CAUTION

Killed. Spiked. Nixed. It doesn't matter what you call it. It is a reality for every editorial cartoonist. In a normal year, the publisher rejected two or three of my cartoons. It's my job to be provocative and push the boundaries, so it only makes sense that some would go too far for management. None of the cartoons in this chapter were published by the *Pittsburgh Post-Gazette*, but some were distributed by my syndicate and appeared on social media.

For example, Pittsburgh is a very Catholic city. When I drew cartoons about any of the Catholic Church's pedophile scandals, the publisher grew nervous. He had received many angry calls from the bishop, not to mention angry letters from Catholic readers.

When Pope Benedict retired in 2013, publisher John Robinson Block was out of the country. It was a monumental story. Never before had a modern-day pope stepped down voluntarily. I had to draw something about it. I imagined seeing the pope do the unemployed walk of shame, carrying all of his office belongings in a box as he leaves the Vatican. I had the cartoon completely inked in when the publisher called in from overseas and killed it. I came up with a second idea that I felt was also good, but a little less brutal. Again, I had it completely inked in by the time the publisher checked in a second time. He killed that one, too. I switched to an idea about Kim Jong Un. That one made the cut.

Two weeks after the 9/11 attacks I tried to remind readers that the U.S. was no angel.
The editors hated it. Too soon, they said. - *September 29, 2001*

The Roman Catholic Archdiocese of Boston agreed to pay $85 million to settle sexual abuse
cases. Meanwhile, the search for bin Laden continued. - *September 11, 2003*

This cartoon was drawn after the White House Correspondent's Dinner where Laura Bush joked that George had "learned a lot about ranching since that first year when he tried to milk the horse." Even I agreed this should not go to print. – May 5, 2005

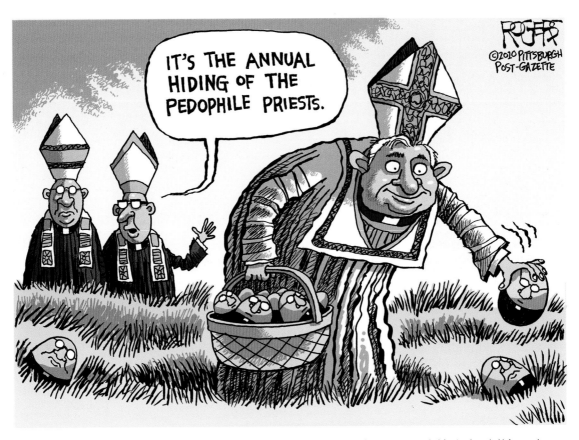

Drawn for use on Good Friday in the midst of news about the church's sex scandal in Ireland, this cartoon was killed at the *Post-Gazette*. A week later, it made the Friday roundup in *USA Today*. – April 3, 2010

Pope Benedict's decision to retire was a historic event.
- *February 14, 2013*

This was my second (unsuccessful) attempt to draw an acceptable cartoon
on the pope's retirement. - *February 14, 2013*

Most pundits predicted a Hillary Clinton victory in 2016. When Trump shocked the world with his win, I couldn't help but think of the famous photo with the "Dewey Defeats Truman" headline. - *November 10, 2016*

The election of a radically different president got me thinking about his possible impact on American retailing. - *November 24, 2016*

I marked the president's six-month anniversary with this cartoon referring to his nuclear threats to North Korea and Iran. The publisher was not amused. – *August 13, 2017*

In 2016, my editor of 12 years, Tom Waseleski, took a moral stand and left the paper rather than bow to the publisher's pressure to endorse Donald Trump. Of the top 100 biggest newspapers in the U.S., only two – the *Las Vegas Review-Journal* and the *Florida Times-Union* in Jacksonville – endorsed Trump. In the end, the *Post-Gazette* didn't endorse either candidate, despite publisher John Robinson Block's desire to support Trump. I knew my days were numbered. I ended up surviving another two years, having only a few cartoons killed.

My publisher made no secret of his admiration for Trump. He was even photographed on Trump's private plane. I sat down with Block once in 2016 and again in 2017 to discuss my Trump cartoons. I made the case that it was my job to cover the president and do the best cartoons I could do. Block wanted friendlier depictions of Trump. I said I couldn't do that and still sleep at night. The issue was left hanging.

Then, in March 2018, things got serious. Block promoted Keith Burris to be editorial director over both papers in the Block chain, the *Pittsburgh Post-Gazette* and *The Blade* of Toledo, Ohio. Burris, who shared the publisher's admiration for Trump, had been the editorial page editor in Toledo and was responsible for writing the "Reason As Racism" editorial that was panned by many as a racist defense of Trump's "shithole countries" comments. Burris was now my boss. From his first week on the job he began killing ideas and finished cartoons. Most years I would have an average of two or three cartoons killed. In the three months that Burris was my editor, he killed 18 cartoons or cartoon ideas. What follows are the first twelve of those cartoons.

This was the first cartoon idea killed by the *Post-Gazette*'s new editorial director, Keith Burris.
My version of Trump's trade war, a la "Apocalypse Now." – *March 5, 2018*

Rick Saccone, the Republican candidate in Pennsylvania's 18th Congressional District, claimed to be Trumpier than Trump, who won that district by 20 points in 2016. Saccone, however, was defeated by Democrat Conor Lamb in the special election. – *March 11, 2018*

The storm over Stormy Daniels was building fast.
- March 18, 2018

Trump continued to malign the FBI, fanning conspiracies of a "deep state"
that was out to get him. *- March 22, 2018*

4-13-18

Neither snow nor rain nor heat nor gloom of night stays these couriers from the swift completion of their appointed rounds ...

... rabid dogs are another story.

The president criticized the U.S. Postal Service for giving discounts to Amazon. That was a two-fer for Trump because Amazon CEO Jeff Bezos also owns *The Washington Post.* - *April 13, 2018*

4-13-18

What if Syrian President Bashar al-Assad, infamous for using chemical weapons on his own people, could advise EPA chief Scott Pruitt on how to roll back federal rules on toxic substances? - *April 13, 2018*

Rather than chart a course of independence on the Russian collusion investigation, House Intelligence Chair Devin Nunes behaved like the head of the Donald Trump Fan Club. - *May 3, 2018*

All the king's fixers and all the king's men ...
are either fired, indicted or on their way to
the pen!

Michael Cohen, the president's loyal fixer, was showing signs of buckling to the pressure of the Mueller probe and telling all. - *May 11, 2018*

Trump marked the one-year anniversary of the Mueller investigation
the only way he knew how, with an angry tweet. – *May 18, 2018*

Despite her past role as chief of a CIA "black site" where prisoners were tortured,
Gina Haspel was confirmed by the Senate as the new head of the CIA. – *May 21, 2018*

After the Gina Haspel sketch was killed, I proposed this cartoon about presidential torture.
- *May 21, 2018*

Roseanne Barr's sitcom, which was cancelled after her racist tweets, was not the only place on TV to see America's divisions. - *May 30, 2018*

Pat Bagley, July 18, 2018

"Freedom of speech" is more than words. It's pictures, too. What people in power do to people who draw funny pictures of them is an important measure of a free and open society. The Association of American Editorial Cartoonists exists to protect the rights of individuals to express themselves through words and pictures, including those that mock the rich and powerful. This exhibit draws attention to one of our members, Rob Rogers, who lost his position at the *Pittsburgh Post-Gazette* for cartoons depicting the president of the United States.

Rob wasn't jailed or physically intimidated, as sometimes happens to cartoonists in other parts of the world who dare challenge the establishment. The management of the *Post-Gazette* was well within its legal rights to fire an employee who didn't reflect its corporate agenda, but it is still troubling that people with a reason to curry favor in Washington, D.C., rid themselves of a popular voice that for 25 years had been an asset to the paper and the political life of Pittsburgh.

By the way, the AAEC also protects the rights of cartoonists to mock the poor and powerless, which may be unseemly, but that is what freedom of speech is all about.

Pat Bagley is the award-winning editorial cartoonist for the *Salt Lake Tribune* and the president of the AAEC. This essay was written for the exhibition *Spiked: The Unpublished Political Cartoons of Rob Rogers* at George Washington University's Corcoran School of the Arts and Design.

7. Trump Year Two: Enemy of the People

President Trump's second year in office looked much like his first: filled with lies, distractions, betrayals, angry tweets and abhorrent behavior.

He continued his efforts to characterize the media as the "enemy of the people" while spewing conspiracy theories and false narratives. He demonized respected agencies like the FBI and the CIA while pardoning criminals and accused child abusers. He separated children from their families at the border while embracing despotic tyrants overseas.

To paraphrase Walt Kelly's Pogo, "We have met the enemy... and he is Trump!"

Trump's lawyer fired off cease-and-desist letters to former advisor Steve Bannon and author Michael Wolff regarding unflattering portrayals of the president in Wolff's book *Fire and Fury.* – *January 7, 2018*

In an Oval Office meeting, the president expressed frustration over immigrants coming to the U.S. from "shithole countries." – *January 18, 2018*

I, Tonya, a movie about figure skater Tonya Harding, offered a metaphor on Trump's knack for skating around controversy. - *January 25, 2018*

When Democrats failed to stand and clap during Trump's State of the Union address he called them "treasonous." - *February 8, 2018*

After barely a year, the Trump White House had become infamous for its
cast of unsavory characters. - *February 9, 2018*

Despite the indictment of 13 Russians for undermining the 2016 election, the president refused to
condemn the threat, insisting only that his campaign had no collusion. - *February 20, 2018*

LAWS

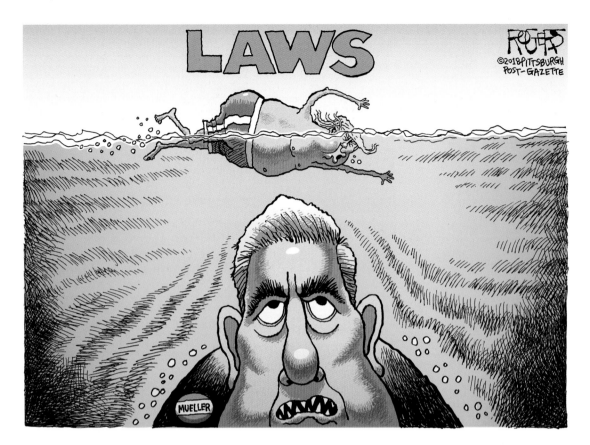

After Robert Mueller issued indictments, 76 percent of Americans said they believed the
Russian government tried to influence the 2016 election. – *March 2, 2018*

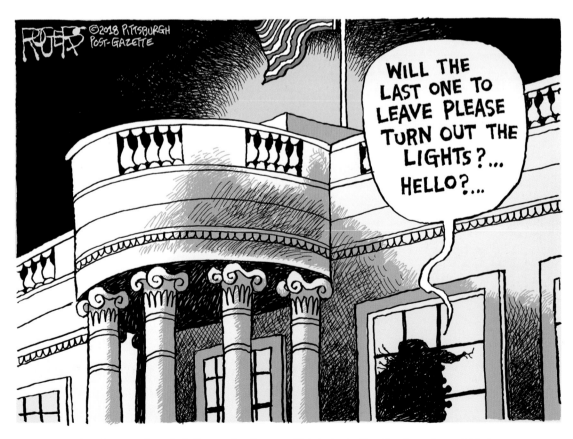

WILL THE LAST ONE TO LEAVE PLEASE TURN OUT THE LIGHTS?... HELLO?...

In a two-week period, five senior Trump officials, including the Secretary of State
and the communications director, left the administration. – *March 8, 2018*

Speaker of the House Paul Ryan, one of the president's highest-ranking Republican apologists, announced he would not run for re-election. – *April 13, 2018*

Was Trump's pardon of Bush-Cheney aide Scooter Libby a smoke signal to Paul Manafort to stay loyal to the president during the Mueller probe? – *April 15, 2018*

Sean Hannity's fealty to Trump was laid bare when he was revealed to be a client of the president's personal lawyer. – *April 20, 2018*

Trump tried to enlist the support of French President Emmanuel Macron by hosting him at an official state visit. – *April 26, 2018*

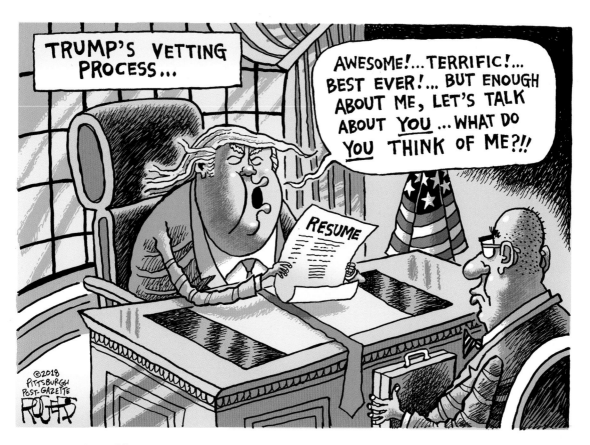

Lax White House vetting of the president's nominees began to frustrate senators.
– *May 3, 2018*

Prior to his summit with Kim Jong Un, Trump welcomed three American detainees
who had been freed by North Korea. – *May 13, 2018*

The president was frustrated and angered by incessant leaks from his administration.
— *May 16, 2018*

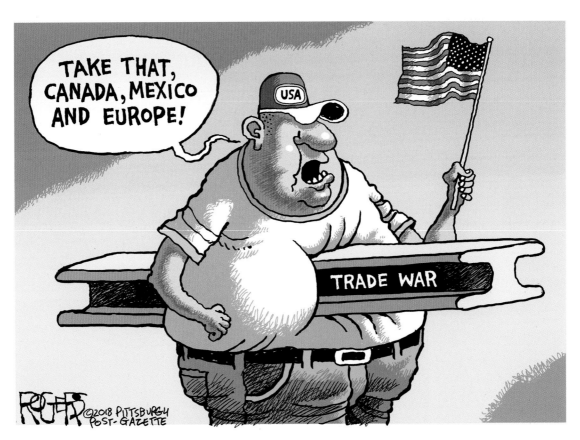

This was my last cartoon published in the *Pittsburgh Post-Gazette*.
An appropriate image for how I was feeling at the time. - *June 5, 2018*

The AAEC Board, June 4, 2018

The longtime cartoonist for the *Pittsburgh Post-Gazette* has gone missing. Actually, we know exactly where Rob Rogers is – at his desk creating the excellent award-winning editorial cartoons he is famous for. But it's those cartoons that have been missing for over a week from the *Post-Gazette* editorial pages, though we know Rob is drawing them because new cartoons are being posted on the web.

It doesn't take much to connect the dots between the absence of Rob's left-leaning cartoons and the recent arrival of a Trump-supporting editorial page editor. We would take this opportunity to remind all editorial page editors that their responsibility is to the readers (among whom in Pittsburgh, Rogers cartoons are wildly popular) and to the open and ongoing search for truth in contending opinions.

The editorial pages are a public forum, not a members-only private resort in Florida.

This statement was issued from the Association of American Editorial Cartoonists issued after six cartoons in a row were killed by the *Pittsburgh Post-Gazette*.

8. Six in a Row? That Has to Be Some Kind of Record!

137

As I was driving to Philadelphia for the 2018 National Cartoonists Society convention on Memorial Day weekend, I received a phone call from a colleague saying the cartoon I had worked on the night before had been killed. I often work ahead when I am leaving town. The cartoon showed President Trump laying a wreath at the tomb of "truth." I had a suspicion this one might be met with some resistance.

I had been working under the enhanced scrutiny and oversight of new editorial director Keith Burris for several months. I arrived at the hotel in time to draw a replacement cartoon. I figured I could always send the Memorial Day cartoon out for syndication, so I quickly drew one about the NFL's decision to have all players stand during the National Anthem. This cartoon, I thought, would be fine. It only tangentially touched on Trump. I was wrong; it, too, was killed. I spent the weekend drinking with my fellow cartoonists, sharing my frustrations, unaware that those two cartoons would be the beginning of the end.

When I returned to Pittsburgh, I drew a cartoon about Starbucks and the NFL. I was convinced this one would be accepted. There was no reference to Trump whatsoever. Killed. Okay, now I was really wondering what was up.

My attempts to get an explanation by phone or email were met with silence. For years I have worked out of my home studio and not in the newsroom. We communicated almost exclusively by email and phone. I would write out my idea in an email to the editorial page editor and publisher in the morning. During normal times (before March of 2018) I would get a response back that said "funny" or "great" or "sounds good." Often I would get feedback on how to improve the idea by changing a word or editing the caption. There was plenty of back and forth discussion and it was a very collaborative process.

In the Burris era this changed dramatically. I would get a simple "no" and when I asked why I would get no response. This was my new reality. I did try to work with them. I changed topics many times and even altered cartoons as long as it did not hurt the integrity of the idea.

By the time the third cartoon in a row was killed, readers noticed the absence of my cartoons in the paper. People began commenting and complaining. Media outlets started calling.

The next day, Wednesday, May 30, all the news coverage was about Roseanne Barr being fired by ABC. My first cartoon idea made a direct comparison between her racist tweets and Trump (see bottom sketch on page 123). It was the perfect comparison. It was killed. By this time I felt as though I was being deliberately pushed out of the paper. I decided to draw a cartoon about Roseanne's Ambien excuse. No mention of Trump. Surely this would get in, I thought. And it did. Burris said okay. The cartoon was finished, put on the page and ready to be printed when the publisher decided to replace it. This was a real gut punch. Why would he do this except as some form of punishment? I was baffled and incensed. I couldn't sleep. I woke up at 5 a.m. the next day and wrote a long email to both John Block and Keith Burris recounting my long career and my great 25-year relationship with the paper. Again, I pleaded for an explanation and offered to talk about solutions to end this standoff. One suggestion I had made several times over the last three months was for them to move my work to the Op-Ed page. That way I could keep my readers happy and they could change the direction of the editorial page to be more pro-Trump. They had ignored that request but I offered it again.

Again, their response was silence. But not from readers and the media. They were getting more and more restless. I knew it would be a waste of time to try to get inside the head of my publisher. I just went back to the drawing board. My next two cartoons were about Trump. Granted, by this time I had given up trying to wait for approval. I never even emailed the ideas. I just drew them. The paper did not print either one.

These six in a row went on to be printed all over the world on social media, blogs, podcasts and news web sites. They were printed in major newspapers and given time on cable news channels. Many more people ended up seeing these killed cartoons than if the *Post-Gazette* had simply published them. Oh, the irony.

The NFL bowed to pressure from the president and decided to require players to stand for the National Anthem. - *May 25, 2018*

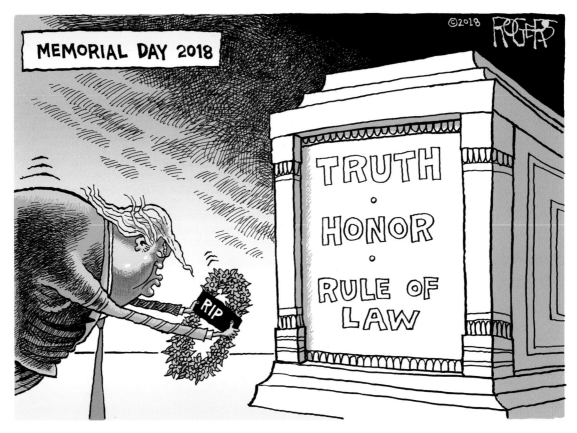

The president declared war with the truth.
It seemed only fitting to have him pay his respects to the fallen. - *May 27, 2018*

Starbucks closed its stores for a day to hold racial sensitivity training.
The NFL did not. – *May 30, 2018*

After being fired from her own show by ABC for sending racist tweets,
Roseanne Barr tried to blame it on taking the sleeping drug Ambien. – *May 31, 2018*

The Trump administration began separating children from their families at the border to send a strong message about illegal immigration. Many called it child abuse. - *June 1, 2018*

After Trump pardoned former Arizona Sheriff Joe Arpaio, late boxing legend Jack Johnson and former Dick Cheney aide Scooter Libby, it appeared as if he was willing to pardon anyone. - *June 3, 2018*

On June 2, WESA, the local NPR station, picked up the news of the killed cartoons and ran a story. Other news outlets followed suit. I refused to comment because I was still employed and did not want to jeopardize any negotiations that might be forthcoming. That didn't stop the media buzz.

Then, after more than a week of killing my cartoons without much communication or explanation, management finally reached out to me. But it wasn't Block or Burris. It was the head of Human Resources, Steve Spolar. He asked me to meet him on Monday to consider a proposal. Not at the paper, but at the law offices of the *Post-Gazette*'s attorneys. I was shocked and offended that they were treating me like some sort of legal threat rather than a dedicated employee doing his job, but anything was better than silence. I said okay.

On Monday, June 4, I drew a cartoon about Trump's steel tariffs and how they would adversely affect workers. I finished the cartoon and drove to the *Post-Gazette*'s attorney's office to meet with Spolar. On my way to meet him I was notified that the tariff cartoon had been approved. Well, that's something, I thought. Maybe this will work out after all. The meeting was brief. Spolar handed me a two-page document and said these were the new "working guidelines" and instructed me to take them with me and read them over carefully. I said I would do that. I glanced at the two pages and saw bullet points defining new rules of my employment. There was also a place for me to sign and date. This was a contract. I said, "These are negotiable, right?" He replied, "No, those are the new guidelines."

When I got home I took a closer look at the document. It had been written by Burris. Not only were the terms not reasonable, they were downright draconian and insulting. The document began with a paragraph insisting that "our conflict here is not about any political litmus test, or politics" and that it is about "working together." All one had to do was look at the cartoons that were killed to know that wasn't accurate.

Further down under the bullet points he chastised me for drawing cartoons that are "not funny or insightful but simply angry and mean" and chided me with phrases like "I have asked many times... that you temper this anger and meanness." Did they really expect me to sign a document that scolded me like a six-year old?

The document went downhill from there. The "new guidelines" consisted of coming into the office every day (that one I could live with), submitting three sketches a day (not unreasonable for someone just starting out, but I knew it would be their way to tamp down my creativity), and, finally, Burris wanted me to work with him to "craft the message acceptable to you and to the publisher." Cartoons by committee? Never a winning formula.

There were 11 bullet points in all, each one more insulting than the one before. I wrote back to Spolar letting him know that the characterization of my work and temperament were false and that the terms were untenable and unacceptable. It was not a contract I could sign. Once again, I pushed for a move to the Op-Ed page or some other solution.

On Tuesday I informed the *Post-Gazette* I would be using vacation days until the issue was resolved. The fact that they suddenly printed one of my cartoons created the false sense that all was back to normal, but if they were insisting that I sign a document like this, then it was clear that they had no interest in working things out. I decided it was time to break my media silence. One of the first people to reach out to me during the week of the killed cartoons was Jake Tapper of CNN. On Wednesday I called him back and said I would gladly go on his show.

The next eight days of waiting was excruciating. I had no idea what the *Post-Gazette* was thinking or what the outcome would be. I continued doing interviews and taking vacation days. The support from the public was amazing. I felt pretty sure the *Post-Gazette* might come back with a more acceptable offer, even if it meant a reduced salary. I received another call from Spolar saying he wanted to see me at the law office on Thursday, June 14.

Once again, the meeting was brief. I was given two documents. One was a severance package and one was a freelance contract. When he handed me the severance package I said, "severance... so this means I'm fired?" He said, "we don't like to say fired, we like to say terminated." I really couldn't believe he was joking about my job loss. Then, in case there was any question that I was no longer employed, he asked me for my *Post-Gazette* ID that had a microchip allowing me access to the building. I took both contracts and left, no longer a *Pittsburgh Post-Gazette* employee.

This time I drove straight to my lawyer's office. He's a labor lawyer who works with many of the unions around Pittsburgh and Western Pennsylvania. He said these were some of the worst labor documents he had ever seen. The severance package would have given me six months pay, but at a cost. It contained a broad non-disparagement agreement. It would have prevented me from talking about my firing or any of the killed cartoons. Then there was a paragraph that claimed ownership of all the cartoons I had ever drawn at the paper, including the ones they did not publish. There was no way I was going to sign a document like this.

The freelance agreement was equally insulting. It offered me $100 a cartoon for three cartoons a week. The contract also stipulated that the *Post-Gazette* would own all of the work done for them and they reserved the right to edit as before, killing cartoons they did not like. If I was not willing to work under those conditions for full salary and benefits, why would I be willing to do it for $100 a cartoon? Once again, it felt like they were not at all serious about keeping me on at the paper, despite what they were saying publicly.

I left the newspaper after 25 years with nothing but my integrity.

Andy Marlette, June 16, 2018

They got another one of us. A cartoonist. Rob Rogers. He drew cartoons critical of the president. So a publisher who puts the American president above American principles (you know, stuff like liberty, individualism and irreverence for government authority figures) fired him last week.

Even if art triumphs in the end, it's important to stand against the common intolerance of true believers who fear the pen and want to kill drawings at all costs.

In Paris they used bullets. In Pittsburgh they used bureaucrats. In Paris they did it for the prophet. In Pittsburgh they did it for the president.

See how easily lines blur for folks who crave subservience and worship authority over morality? Which is why the clarity of cartoon lines is a virtue in this world. Because when you stare at a photograph of a president smiling and schmoozing and standing shoulder to shoulder with a murderous tyrant, it's almost impossible to recognize our nation's founding principles, faith and values.

But when you look at the lines inked by folks like Rob Rogers, what truly makes America great couldn't be clearer.

It's the symbolism, stupid. And in these strange American days we're living in, a crackdown on cartoonists is no coincidence.

Andy Marlette is the editorial cartoonist for the *Pensacola* (Fla.) *News Journal*. This first appeared in his paper.

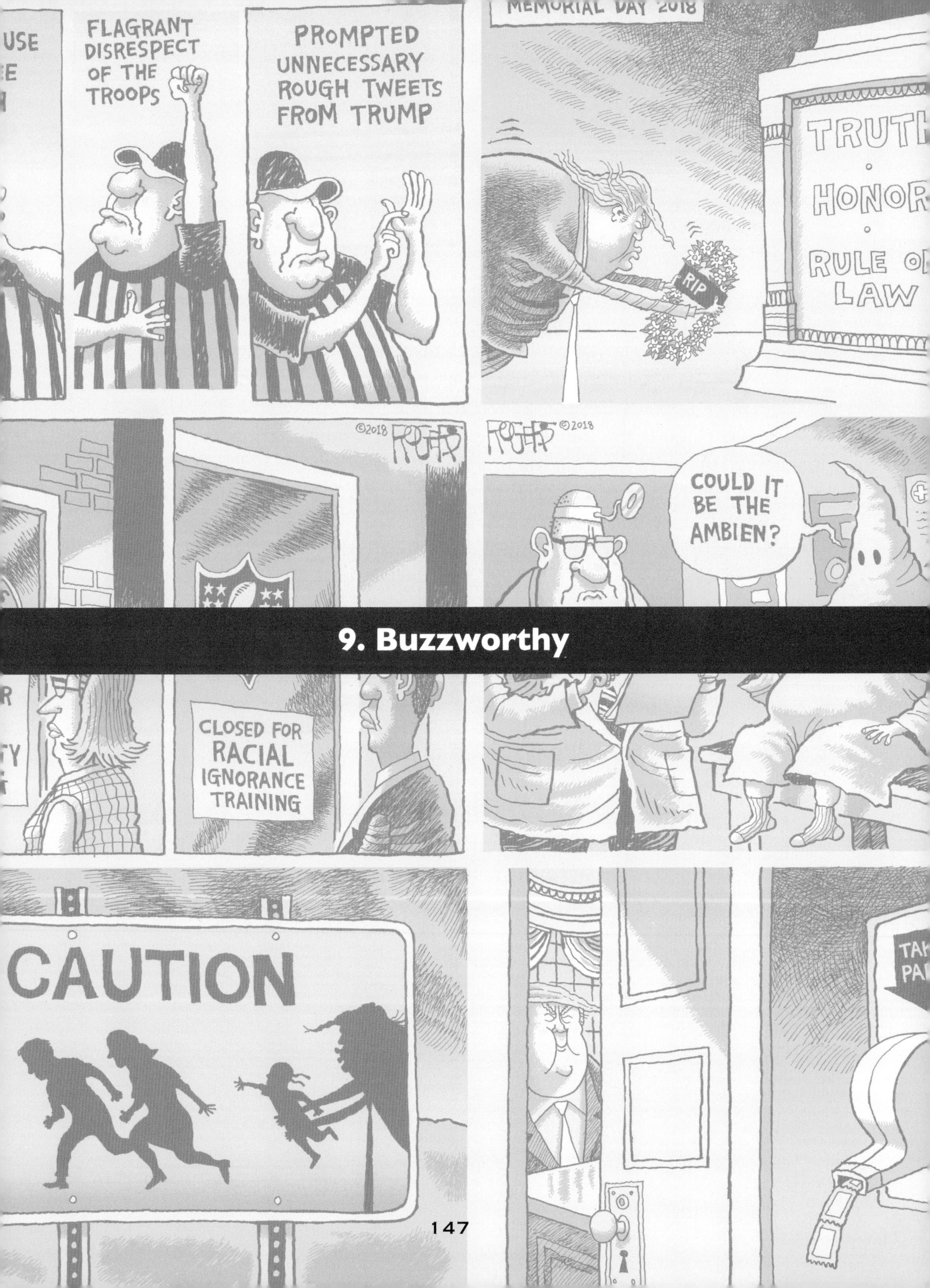
FLAGRANT DISRESPECT OF THE TROOPS
PROMPTED UNNECESSARY ROUGH TWEETS FROM TRUMP
MEMORIAL DAY 2018
TRUT
HONOR
RULE O
LAW
RIP
©2018
COULD IT BE THE AMBIEN?
CLOSED FOR RACIAL IGNORANCE TRAINING
CAUTION

9. Buzzworthy

From the moment my Facebook friends and Twitter followers started noticing that I was posting cartoons that had not appeared in the paper, the buzz began. People theorized why they weren't being printed and they began sharing the killed cartoons. By the time the fourth cartoon in a row was killed, I was forced to admit on social media that, yes indeed, management had been killing the cartoons.

That's when the whole thing took off. It was only a matter of hours before news outlets were calling to talk. I still had no idea why they were killing the cartoons or what their plan was so I remained the faithful employee and did not talk to the media. I continued to reach out to management with the hopes of meeting and discussing options, like moving my cartoons to the Op-Ed page. No response. The media continued to print the news of my cartoons being spiked from the paper.

I was shocked by the amount of media coverage my story generated. It was comforting to know that other journalists and media outlets found the circumstances of my firing disturbing. I was also touched and overwhelmed by the public support from fans and followers on social media. Here are just a few of the stories, tweets and photos that popped up before and after I was fired.

Pittsburgh Post-Gazette Editorial Page Not Publishing Longtime Cartoonist's Recent Work

By LUCY PERKINS & CHRIS POTTER · JUN 2, 2018

 Tweet　 Share　 Google+　✉ Email

Chris Potter, a former colleague from the *Post-Gazette*, now at public radio station WESA-FM, was the first to call.
- June 2, 2018

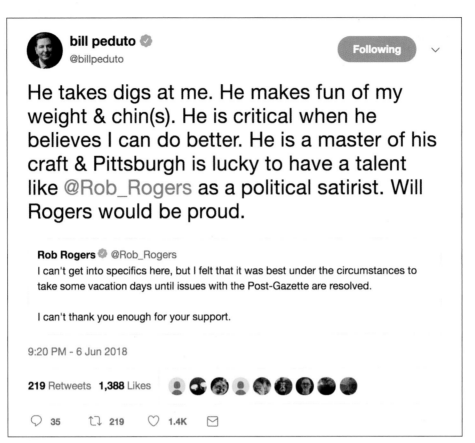

Pittsburgh Mayor Bill Peduto, who has been the subject of many of my cartoons,
nevertheless voiced his support on Twitter. - *June 6, 2018*

Here is an earlier cartoon I drew about the mayor.
He was responding to candidate Trump's attack on sanctuary cities. - *December 20, 2015*

Award-Winning Editorial Cartoonist's Often Liberal Cartoons Absent From Post-Gazette's Pages

By Jon Delano   June 4, 2018 at 6:26 pm   Filed Under: Jon Delano, Local TV, Pittsburgh Post-Gazette, Rob Rogers

Follow KDKA-TV: Facebook | Twitter

KDKA, the local CBS affiliate, was the next one to report the story of the killed cartoons. KDKA is the local news partner of the *Post-Gazette*, so this story made some producers a little nervous. – *June 4, 2018*

FAIR Challenging media bias since 1986.

ABOUT ⌄   ISSUES & STUDIES ⌄   COUNTERSPIN PODCAST ⌄   EXTRA! NEWSLETTER ⌄   TAKE ACTION ⌄   STORE   DON

JUNE 6, 2018

Anti-Trump Cartoons Stopped by Censor at Pittsburgh Post-Gazette

OLIVIA RIGGIO

FAIR, the national media watch group, picked up the story.
– *June 6, 2018*

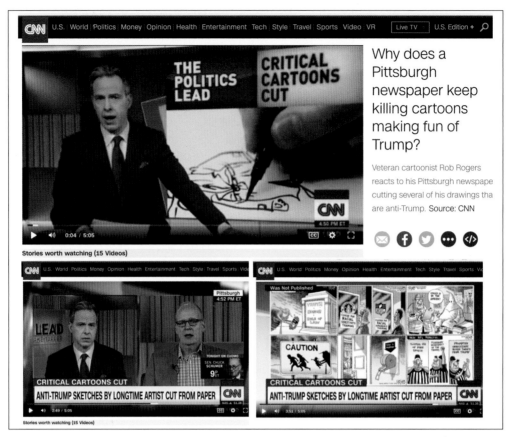

I broke my media silence by going on CNN's "The Lead with Jake Tapper."
Jake is a political cartoonist in his own right, so I felt like he would understand. – *June 6, 2018*

Barbra Streisand was upset that my publisher was raining on my parade. How cool is that?
– *June 7, 2018*

Comic Riffs

Pittsburgh Post-Gazette cartoonist is seeing many anti-Trump cartoons spiked

By **Michael Cavna**, Writer/artist
June 8

ROB ROGERS has been a Pittsburgh editorial cartoonist for 34 years — for the past quarter-century at the Pittsburgh Post-Gazette. And during that long run, he says, he's had only two to three cartoons a year, on average, killed by his editors.

Since March of this year, though, he says he's had nine cartoon ideas killed and 10 finished cartoons spiked — six of those between May 25 and June 4, when, he says, not a single one of his cartoons was deemed worthy of publishing in the Post-Gazette.

One of Rob Rogers's finished cartoons that was recently killed by his Pittsburgh Post-Gazette editors. (Rob Rogers/Andrews McMeel Syndication)

"The Post-Gazette finally published one of my cartoons [this week] for the first time since May 24," Rogers tells The Washington Post's Comic Riffs. "Due to the fact that things were still unresolved with management, I decided to take personal days for the

The Washington Post, which has the slogan "Democracy Dies in Darkness," noticed that my cartoons were not seeing the light of day. – *June 8, 2018*

Pittsburgh radio personality Lynn Cullen organized a "Support Rob Rogers" rally using blowups of my cartoons. (Video still and photo courtesy of John Harvey.) – *June 10, 2018*

Poynter.

Ethics　Fact-Checking　Innovation　Digital Tools　Leadership

STORYTELLING | Detail from a Rob Rogers editorial cartoon June 3 that was spiked by the Pittsburgh Post-Gazette. (Used with permission).

Pittsburgh paper fires longtime editorial cartoonist after dispute over Trump work

BY DAVID BEARD · JUNE 14, 2018

  　　TAGS:　Editorial cartooning

A editorial shift toward President Trump preceded the firing, and raises questions of editorial independence in Pittsburgh and elsewhere

Rob Rogers says he saw it coming.

A new editorial page chief had come to the Pittsburgh Post-Gazette with the support of the newspaper's owner, a supporter of President Trump. Rogers, the paper's highly regarded editorial cartoonist for the past quarter-century, suddenly started seeing his cartoons being rejected for print.

The Poynter Institute for Media Studies, which focuses on ethics in journalism and reports on the media, said my firing raised questions of editorial independence. *- June 14, 2018*

Columbia Journalism Review.

The voice of journalism

Local News   **Covering Trump**   **Business of Journalism**   **Innovation**   About   Donate   Membership   Magazine   Advertise   Contact

What the world needs now.

Join CJR and help journalism be at its best »

**UNITED STATES
PROJECT**

In Pittsburgh, an unprecedented blow to editorial cartoonist

By Kim Lyons

JUNE 11, 2018
1453 WORDS

**SHARE
ON TWITTER**

©2018 Rob Rogers. Reprinted with permission.

UPDATE: Rob Rogers, a *Post-Gazette* editorial cartoonist for more than two decades, says he has been fired from the paper. Rogers' announcement comes after the *Post-Gazette* declined to run a number of Rogers' cartoons, and more than a week after the paper posted a Rogers cartoon on its

What the world needs now.

As an independent non-profit, the Columbia Journalism Review is in a unique position to help journalism be at its best. But we can't do it alone.

Columbia Journalism Review ran a story about the killed cartoons and then updated it after I was fired. - *June 11, 2018*

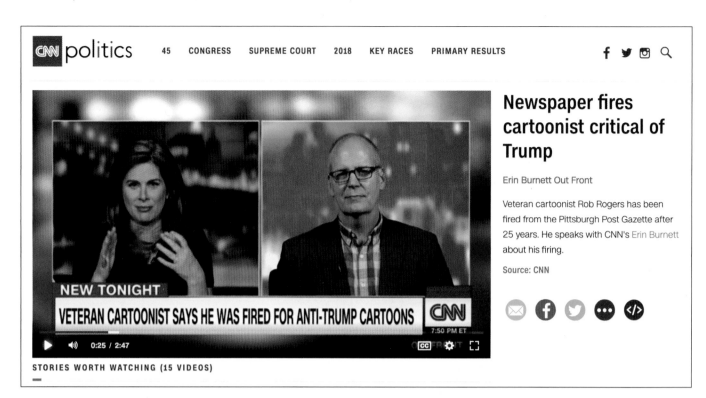

Newspaper fires cartoonist critical of Trump

Erin Burnett Out Front

Veteran cartoonist Rob Rogers has been fired from the Pittsburgh Post Gazette after 25 years. He speaks with CNN's Erin Burnett about his firing.

Source: CNN

After I was fired, it was back to CNN, this time with Erin Burnett.
- June 14, 2018

Robert Reich
Like This Page · June 15 · 🌐

Rob Rogers, editorial cartoonist for the Pittsburgh Post-Gazette, was fired Thursday because the publisher is pro-Trump and Rogers had been submitting cartoons critical of Trump. Memo to publisher: Freedom of speech and of the press includes cartooning. Memo to the good people of Pittsburgh: Cancel your subscriptions.

👍😠😮 32K   1.6K Comments 18K Shares

👍 Like   💬 Comment   ↪ Share

Political commentator Robert Reich weighed in with a post on his Facebook page.
– June 15, 2018

Opinion

I Was Fired for Making Fun of Trump

By Rob Rogers
Mr. Rogers joined The Pittsburgh Post-Gazette as an editorial cartoonist in 1993. He worked there until this week. In 1999, he was a finalist for the Pulitzer Prize.

June 15, 2018   f   🐦   ✉   ➦   🔖

Rob Rogers

After 25 years as the editorial cartoonist for The Pittsburgh Post-Gazette, I was fired on Thursday.

I blame Donald Trump.

Well, sort of.

The New York Times called me hours after I was fired and asked me to write about it for the Sunday Review section. – *June 15, 2018*

George Takei, who portrayed helmsman Hikaru Sulu on "Star Trek," beamed up his support.
- June 15, 2018

The *Post-Gazette* claimed that I wasn't fired because of Trump. Then the publisher contradicted the company line, saying that it was about Trump. *- June 16, 2018*

My immigration cartoon was projected on the side of the San Francisco Federal Building.
(Photo courtesy of ResistanceSF.) *– June 19, 2018*

The Daily Beast asked if I was really that "angry."
– June 20, 2018

Protesters in San Diego marching against Trump's immigration crackdown
used my cartoon on posters. (Photo courtesy of Claire Condra.) - *June 23, 2018*

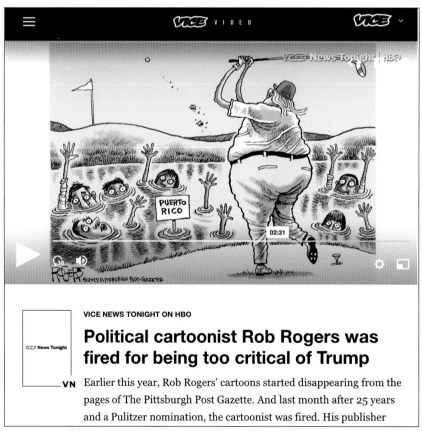

VICE NEWS TONIGHT ON HBO

**Political cartoonist Rob Rogers was
fired for being too critical of Trump**

Earlier this year, Rob Rogers' cartoons started disappearing from the
pages of The Pittsburgh Post Gazette. And last month after 25 years
and a Pulitzer nomination, the cartoonist was fired. His publisher

I gave HBO's "Vice News" a rare, inside look at my studio during an interview after the firing.
- *July 10, 2018*

The Art of a Fired Cartoonist

What if we interpret Rob Rogers's wild art cartoons as if they were conventional subjects for art writing?

David Carrier   July 21, 2018   f y ✉ 483 Shares

Rob Rogers, "Immigrant Children" (June 1, 2018)

Mary Cassatt was born in Pittsburgh; Andy Warhol, also born here, went to school here as well, as did Mel Bochner and Deborah Kass. And over the years a great many major artists have been shown in the Carnegie Museum, in the Internationals and also in other major shows. I know, for I live here, and so have regularly reviewed these exhibitions.

But by miles the most visible Pittsburgh artist is someone who, though his work has appeared for many years regularly in the main local newspaper, *The Pittsburgh Post-Gazette*, has never been shown in that museum. I confess, indeed, that though long ago he took one of my classes, I've never written about his work, though I see his art regularly in that paper. Indeed, only an accident of family life — my daughter Liz's fascination with *Tintin* , the series of comics by the Belgian artist Hergé— got me to seriously thinking about comics art, and publishing a book about them. It's all too easy to ignore what's right at hand.

Art writer and philosophy professor David Carrier wrote a piece for *Hyperallergic* in which he mentioned me in the same breath with Pittsburgh artists Andy Warhol and Mary Cassatt. That's rare company. *- July 21, 2018*

Sanjit Sethi, July 18, 2018

Artists have always been at the forefront of cultural and institutional critique. They produce work that is intended to make us think, that can sometimes make us feel uncomfortable, and that provides searing commentary on the way the world operates. For the institutions like the Corcoran, remaining silent in the face of censorship of creative practices is not an option for our community as it only condones the increasingly insidious and repressive measures we see being enacted on those who voice criticism or dissent.

Rob Rogers is a skilled practitioner who has a remarkable ability to provide the viewer social commentary through the lens of his timely and piercing illustrations. By showing his original work alongside his process sketches and his larger, color-saturated, digitized work, we have the ability to see more than his unpublished cartoons but gain keen insight into his practice. We can more clearly understand that these works are the result of decades of persistent practice. This work gives our community deep insight into creative methodologies on how to critique power and becomes a powerful point of departure for this community to speak with each other about issues around censorship, freedom of the press and artistic expression, journalistic and creative integrity and the consequences of hyper-nationalism to a democracy.

It is clear that Rob Rogers exemplifies that idea of an "American genius" that the Corcoran was founded on. He provides us with that ability to witness that powerful intersection between creativity, social critique, satire, humor and our darkest selves.

Sanjit Sethi is the director of the Corcoran School of the Arts and Design. This essay was written for the exhibition *Spiked: The Unpublished Political Cartoons of Rob Rogers* at George Washington University's Corcoran School of the Arts and Design.

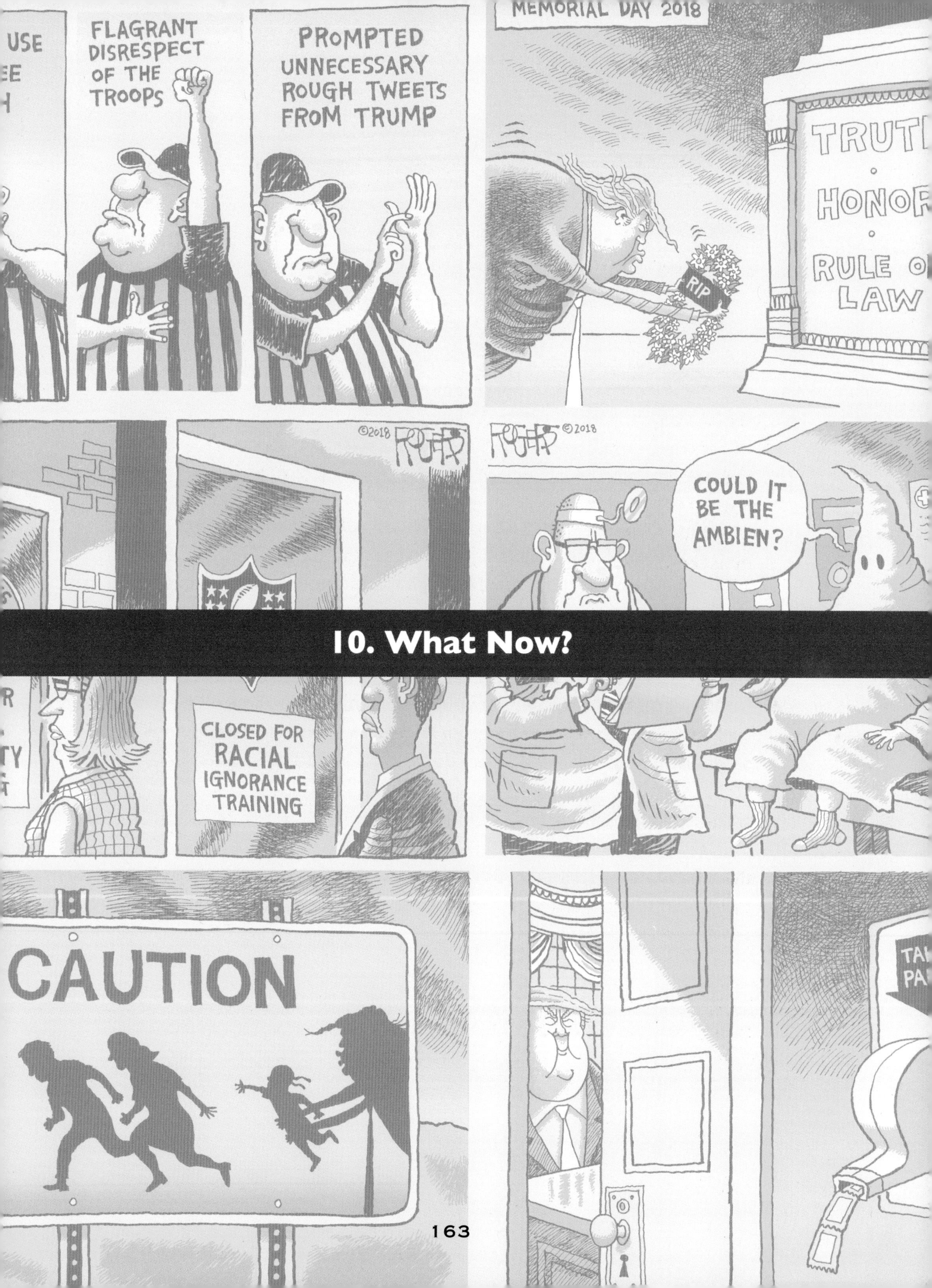
FLAGRANT DISRESPECT OF THE TROOPS
PROMPTED UNNECESSARY ROUGH TWEETS FROM TRUMP
MEMORIAL DAY 2018
RIP
©2018 ROGERS
ROGERS ©2018
COULD IT BE THE AMBIEN?
CLOSED FOR RACIAL IGNORANCE TRAINING
CAUTION

10. What Now?

Everybody thinks about it. We all wonder: what would I do if I wasn't doing this? Climb Everest? Write the great American novel? Watch more Netflix? It's a whole different exercise when the rug gets pulled out from under you before you're ready.

Being fired can really rock your self-worth. Especially when it's a nasty firing. Especially when it's the only job you've ever known and it's inextricably tied to your identity. The good news is, when you have overwhelming support from family, friends and fans, it makes facing the "what now" question a little easier.

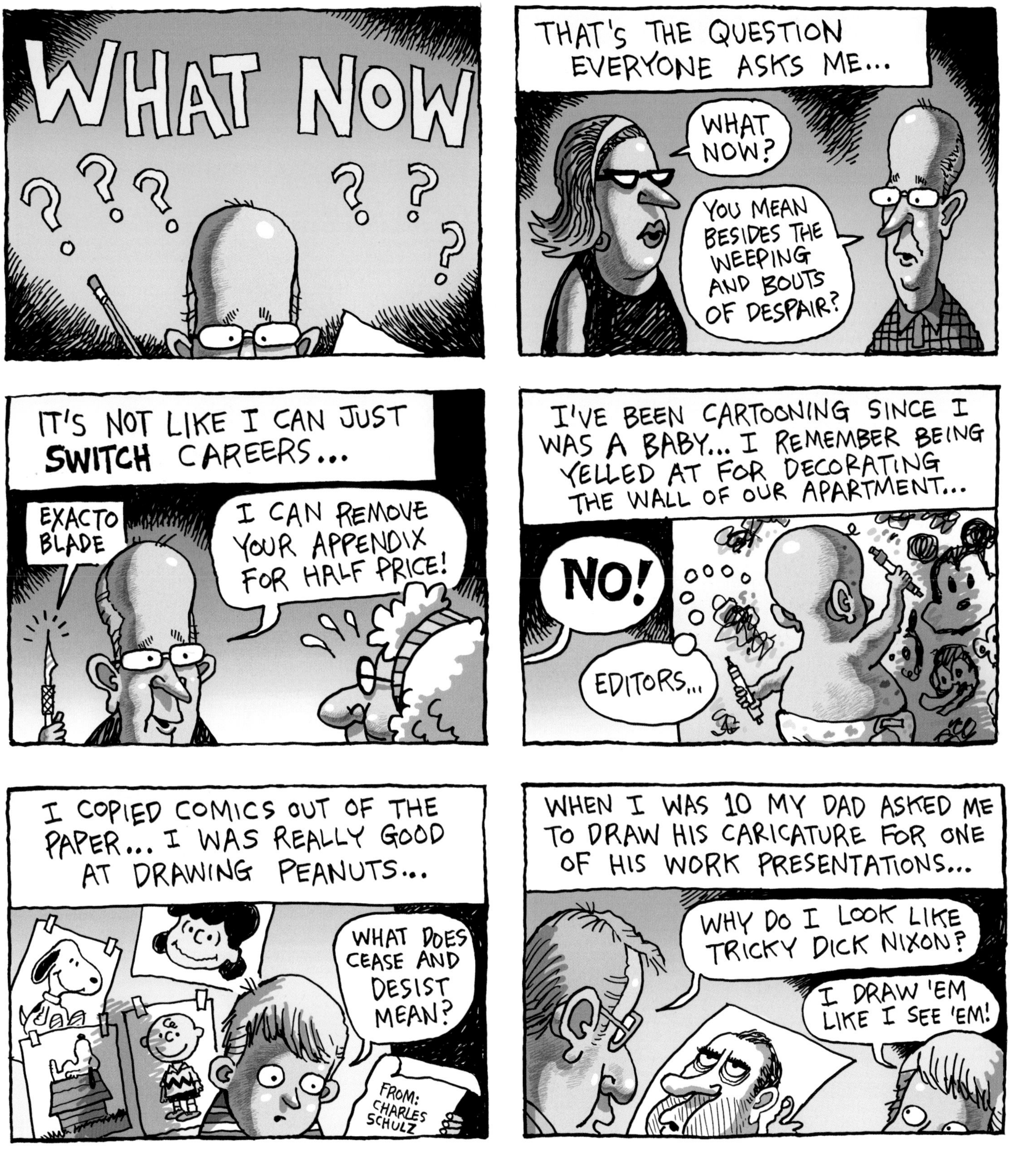
WHAT NOW
THAT'S THE QUESTION EVERYONE ASKS ME...
WHAT NOW?
YOU MEAN BESIDES THE WEEPING AND BOUTS OF DESPAIR?
IT'S NOT LIKE I CAN JUST SWITCH CAREERS...
EXACTO BLADE
I CAN REMOVE YOUR APPENDIX FOR HALF PRICE!
I'VE BEEN CARTOONING SINCE I WAS A BABY... I REMEMBER BEING YELLED AT FOR DECORATING THE WALL OF OUR APARTMENT...
NO!
EDITORS...
I COPIED COMICS OUT OF THE PAPER... I WAS REALLY GOOD AT DRAWING PEANUTS...
WHAT DOES CEASE AND DESIST MEAN?
FROM: CHARLES SCHULZ
WHEN I WAS 10 MY DAD ASKED ME TO DRAW HIS CARICATURE FOR ONE OF HIS WORK PRESENTATIONS...
WHY DO I LOOK LIKE TRICKY DICK NIXON?
I DRAW 'EM LIKE I SEE 'EM!

BY THE TIME I GOT TO COLLEGE MY PATH WAS CLEAR...

WE'LL PAY YOU TO DRAW EDITORIAL CARTOONS FOR THE COLLEGE PAPER.

CALL THE NURSE... I THINK HE FAINTED!

I SPENT THE NEXT THREE DECADES PERFECTING MY CRAFT...

BEATS GETTING A REAL JOB!

IT'S NOT **EXACTLY** AN EASILY TRANSFERABLE **SKILL SET**...

?

WILL **RIDICULE** THOSE IN POWER WITH FUNNY DRAWING AND BITING SATIRE **FOR FOOD!**

SURE, I CAN **DRAW**... BUT MY **ART** ISN'T FOR EVERYONE...

DON'T YOU LOVE THE WAY I PAINTED THE GREEDY CORPORATE POLLUTERS DESCENDING INTO HELL?

YEAH... BUT IS IT RIGHT FOR THE NURSERY?

WITH **NEWSPAPERS** STRUGGLING, BELIEVING I WOULD LAND ANOTHER **STAFF JOB** IS LIKE BELIEVING IN **SANTA CLAUS**...

TODAY: SANTA CLAUS TRYOUTS

HO, HO HO?

I SUPPOSE I COULD APPLY TO BE A **GREETER** AT **WALMART**...

WELCOME TO WALMART... WHERE OUR GOODS ARE MADE IN **CHINA** AND WE DON'T PAY A LIVING WAGE!

WAL★MART

YOU'RE FIRED!

OR A **BARISTA** AT STARBUCKS...

YOU MISSPELLED MY NAME <u>AND</u> YOU MADE MY **NOSE** TOO **BIG!**

I SAID **NO** CARICATURES... YOU'RE **FIRED!**

JON

OR MAYBE I CAN TAKE THAT **ROAD TRIP** I NEVER TOOK AFTER **COLLEGE**...

WELCOME TO XENOPHOBIA USA

IT MIGHT GIVE ME INSIGHT INTO **WHY** ALL OF THIS HAPPENED...

DO YOU THINK SATIRE IS IMPORTANT IN A DEMOCRACY?

SATIRE... IS THAT LIKE FAKE NEWS?

OR MAYBE I CAN GO TO A **MOUNTAINTOP** IN SEARCH OF SPIRITUAL GUIDANCE...

WHAT KIND OF PEN SHOULD I USE?

?

"WHAT NOW?" ISN'T JUST A QUESTION FOR A RECENTLY FIRED **CARTOONIST**...

IT'S A QUESTION FOR **EVERY CITIZEN** WHO CARES ABOUT THE **SOUL** OF AMERICA...

YOU MEAN THE **SOUL** WE SOLD TO **PUTIN?**

Despite being laid off midway through the year, I continue to draw cartoons every week for syndication. I also post my cartoons on Twitter and Facebook and I have started a Patreon page as a way for fans to support me and be a part of my process. I'm still in the trenches, still fighting the good fight, only now the trenches are located on the interwebs.

Here are a few of the cartoons I have drawn since being fired in June 2018.

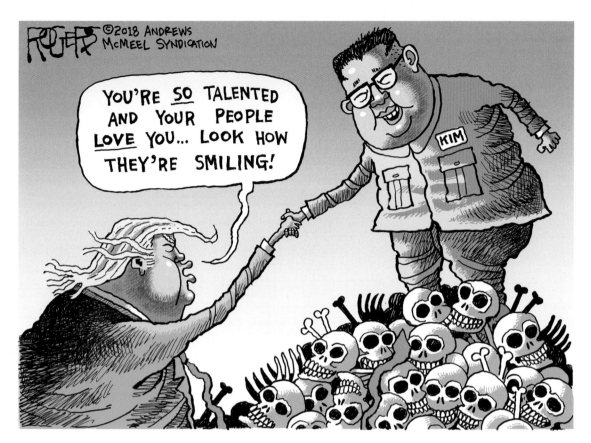

Given Trump's suddenly effusive praise of Kim, it was worth reminding readers of the North Korean's brutal record. I drew this two days before I was fired, for syndication only. – *June 13, 2018*

This is the first cartoon I drew as a freelancer after my firing by the *Post-Gazette*. – *June 19, 2018*

The retirement of Justice Anthony Kennedy gave Trump his second Supreme Court vacancy to fill and a chance to reshape the court for a generation. - *June 29, 2018*

Discredited EPA chief Scott Pruitt resigned after ethics scandals, but not before he was able to roll back environmental standards. - *July 6, 2018*

Harsh treatment of immigrant children who were separated from their families provoked calls for the abolition of the Immigration and Customs Enforcement agency. - *July 7, 2018*

The president's fawning attention toward Kim Jong Un and Vladimir Putin gave credibility to two brutal despots. - *July 10, 2018*

The consensus on the U.S.-Russia summit was unanimous, except in the White House:
Putin scored big at Trump's expense. – *July 17, 2018*

In one of the most remarkable moments in presidential history, Trump stood next to Vladimir Putin and
rejected the view of his intelligence agencies that Russia hacked the 2016 election. – *July 18, 2018*

After the Helsinki summit debacle, Trump tried to say he misspoke when he covered for Putin.
A day later he called the Russian probe a hoax again. - *July 21, 2018*

The plot thickened when a Russian spy surfaced after cozying up to the NRA,
one of Trump's staunchest political allies. - *July 24, 2018*

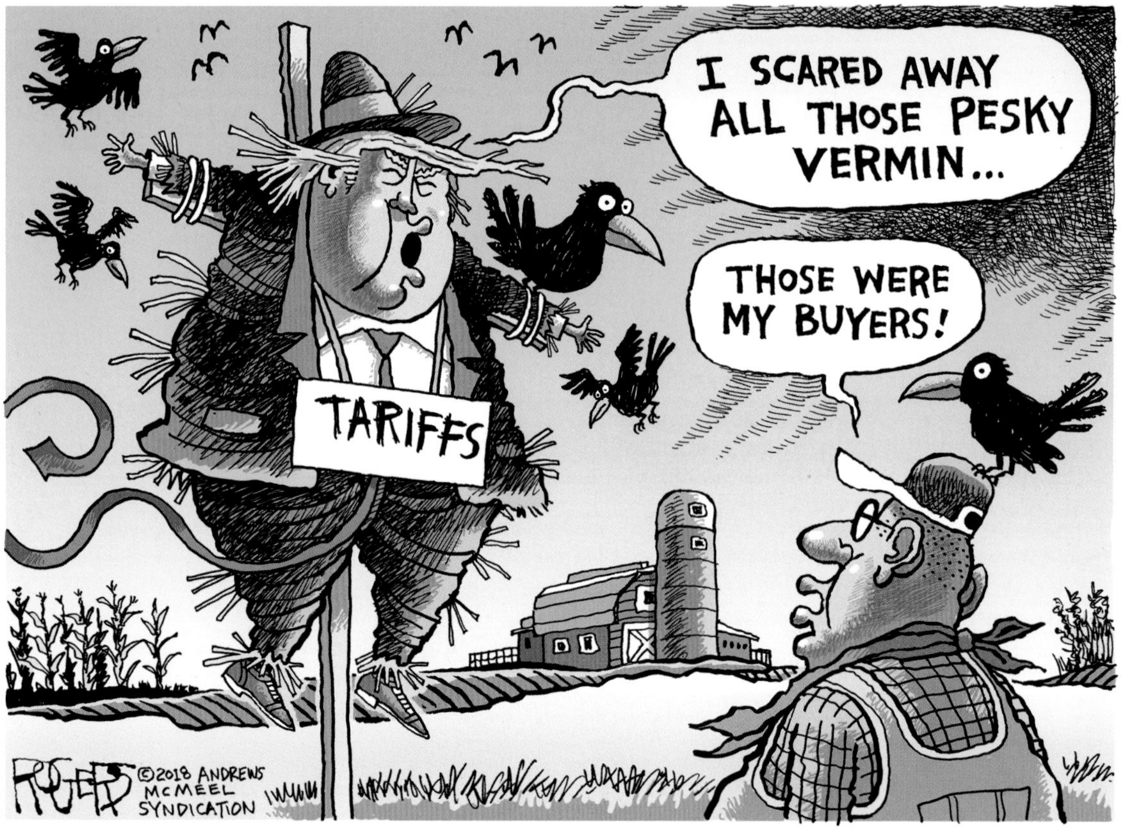
I SCARED AWAY ALL THOSE PESKY VERMIN...
THOSE WERE MY BUYERS!
TARIFFS
ROGERS ©2018 ANDREWS McMEEL SYNDICATION

By summer, farmers and other American producers were feeling the sting of Trump's trade war. - *July 28, 2018*

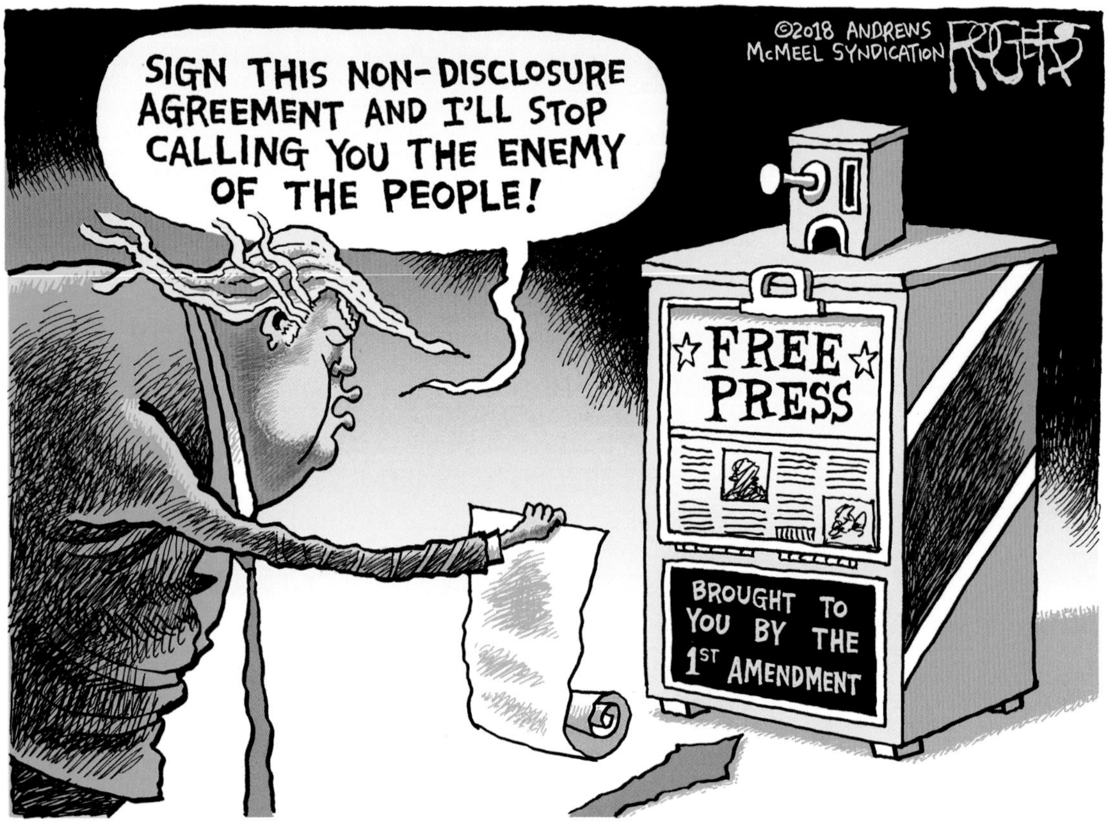
©2018 ANDREWS McMEEL SYNDICATION ROGERS
SIGN THIS NON-DISCLOSURE AGREEMENT AND I'LL STOP CALLING YOU THE ENEMY OF THE PEOPLE!
FREE PRESS
BROUGHT TO YOU BY THE 1ST AMENDMENT

More than 300 news outlets across the country, along with many cartoonists, joined *The Boston Globe* to defend the free press and condemn Trump's attacks on the media. - *August 15, 2018*

ACKNOWLEDGMENTS

Special thanks to my best editor **Sylvia Rhor**. There's no one I'd rather share this crazy ride with. You make me a better person every day.

This book would not have been possible without the generous support of the following people:

Tom Waseleski, for your friendship, patience, wise counsel, sense of humor and years of collaboration. You helped raise my cartoons to another level.

Ann Telnaes, for being more involved in this drama than you ever intended. Your friendship and advice have been invaluable.

Dennis Roddy, we will always have Atlanta 1988.

Joel Pett, the Gallant to my Goofus.

Steve Brodner, you continue to inspire me with your work and your integrity, you bastard.

Pat Bagley, you will always be my preferred president.

David Fitzsimmons, the ultimate muckraking ink-slinger.

Andy Marlette, for standing up for the craft like nobody else. Doug would be proud.

Sanjit Sethi, the best new friend a fired cartoonist could have. I highly recommend an exhibition at the Corcoran for anyone questioning his or her place in the world.

Matt Bors, founder and editor of The Nib, for helping to keep satire alive for future generations.

John Glynn and **Andrews McMeel Syndication**, for your unwavering support of cartoonists and their work, especially mine.

The Association of American Editorial Cartoonists, you will always be my second family. Can't wait for the next dysfunctional family reunion.

Cartoonist Rights Network International, for your ongoing battle for justice for persecuted cartoonists all over the world.

And finally, a big thanks to all of my **friends and fans** out there. Whether in person, by phone, email, social media, or through Patreon, you have supported me in more ways than you will ever know.

Rob Rogers is the award-winning, nationally-syndicated editorial cartoonist formerly with the *Pittsburgh Post-Gazette*. He began his political cartooning career in 1984 at the *Pittsburgh Press*. Nine years later Rogers joined the *Post-Gazette*.

Distributed by Andrews McMeel Syndication, Rogers' work has appeared in *The New York Times*, *The Washington Post*, *USA Today*, *Time*, *Newsweek* and *The Week*, among others.

Rogers is an active member (and past president) of the Association of American Editorial Cartoonists. Rogers' work received the 1995 National Headliner Award, as well as the 2000 and 2013 Thomas Nast Award from the Overseas Press Club. In 2015, Rogers was awarded the Berryman Award from the National Press Foundation. In 1999, he was a finalist for the Pulitzer Prize.

Rogers served as president of the ToonSeum, a museum of comic and cartoon art in Pittsburgh, from 2007 to 2017.

In 2009, Rogers celebrated 25 years as a Pittsburgh editorial cartoonist with the release of his book, *No Cartoon Left Behind: The Best of Rob Rogers*, published by Carnegie Mellon University Press. In 2015, he released a local cartoon collection called, *Mayoral Ink: Cartooning Pittsburgh's Mayors*.

In June of 2018, after 25 years on staff at the *Pittsburgh Post-Gazette*, Rogers was fired for drawing cartoons critical of President Trump.

For more about Rob Rogers go to **www.robrogers.com.** You can follow him on Twitter @Rob_Rogers or support him at https://www.patreon.com/robrogers